D0285292

❝ *Jesus said, 'Let the little children come to me, and do not hinder them, for the kingdom of heaven belongs to such as these.'* **❞**

— *Matthew 19:14 (NIV)*

WHERE DOES GOD LIVE?

Fifty-Eight More
"Something for the Kids"
Children's Sermons
for Worship

TED LAZICKI

MERIWETHER PUBLISHING LTD.
Colorado Springs, Colorado

Meriwether Publishing Ltd., Publisher
Box 7710
Colorado Springs, CO 80933

Editor: Arthur L. Zapel, Rhonda Wray
Typesetting: Sharon E. Garlock
Cover design and illustrations: Michelle Z. Gallardo

© Copyright MCMXCI Meriwether Publishing Ltd.
Printed in the United States of America
First Edition

All rights reserved. No part of this publication may be reproduced, stored in a retrieval system, or transmitted, in any form or by any means, electronic, mechanical, photocopying, recording, or otherwise, without permission of the publishers.

Library of Congress Cataloging-in-Publication Data

Lazicki, Ted.
    Where does God live? : 58 more "Something for the kids" children's
sermons for worship / by Ted Lazicki.
       p.   cm.
    ISBN 0-916260-77-1 : $8.95
    1. Children's sermons. 2. Sermons, American. 3. Church of the
Lutheran Brethren--Sermons. 4. Lutheran Church--Sermons.
I. Title.
BV4315.L35   1991
252'.53--dc20   91-8734
                                          CIP

All Scripture quotations in this publication are from the Holy Bible, New International Version. Copyright © 1973, 1978, 1984, International Bible Society. Used by permission.

Dedication

*To Fern, my precious wife and sweetheart,
who has kept me young down through
these many years.*

*To Peggy Hunerwadel: She and husband Carl
are Bible and Missions students at the
William Carey International University.
Peggy came along, an angel of mercy,
to type this manuscript when I despaired
of getting it done in time. This she did while
home-schooling five children in their
two dormitory rooms on the campus.*

*To the wonderful kids at Immanuel Church,
who run down the aisle each Sunday for the
children's story time. How this warms my heart,
and I must confess, my ego.*

TABLE OF CONTENTS

III. WHAT WE DO FOR OTHERS

IV. LIFE AS A CHRISTIAN

V. SIN, CONFESSION AND FORGIVENESS

VI. THE BIBLE

VII. HOLIDAYS AND SPECIAL USE

INTRODUCTION

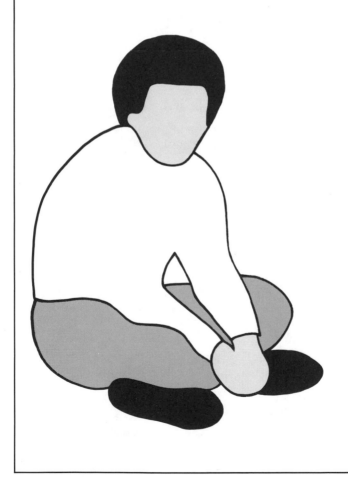

L ong after the church got beyond the "children should be seen and not heard" era, it still did not, for the most part, see the wisdom and the necessity of providing for the little ones something beyond boredom and a church bulletin to scribble on during the morning worship service. Now more and more churches are setting aside a time just for the kids during the worship. I trust the stories that follow will make this time more enjoyable and profitable for them, and prove a real boon to those who have taken upon themselves (or have had it put upon them) to minister to the children during the "storytime for the kids."

If a 30-year effort in this ministry gives one some validity, I offer these suggestions:

Who should be the storyteller? One obvious choice would be the pastor. But he may well not be the best choice. He has plenty to occupy his mind and heart, and may not need this addition — indeed, may have no gift for it. Deliver the kids from one who is doing this simply because "it's his job." The kids deserve the best the church has.

Find one who, of course, loves and relates well to the children; one with a dramatic bent, who can tell the stories without embarrassment, using gestures, facial expressions, and, at times, even costumes, that will delight and capture their minds and hearts.

There is no place for dignity here, or self-consciousness. Ignore the fact that the adults are present. This time belongs to the kids. However, while you ignore the adults, be assured they won't be ignoring you. Though occasionally I may have an inattentive child, I've never noticed an inattentive adult. You have a marvelous time to minister to those in the congregation who become suddenly "hearing impaired" when the sermon of the day touches a sensitive area in their lives which they don't want to deal with. The children's story can blind-side them, and they will be spoken to with a directness and clarity they can't avoid.

I believe the children should sit in the front pew during this time. While the parents may enjoy seeing the children sitting on the platform, it has several disadvantages, the principal one being that the children's attention is harder to capture when they have more than just the storyteller to look at, and they are more likely to act in an attention-getting way, making the teller's task more difficult.

Make your stories as personal as possible. Use names, places, and situations with which the children are familiar. Involve the children by asking questions, but be aware that this has its pitfalls. Don't feel you have to respond to a comment or answer a question they might offer which would tend to take you off in a direction you're not planning to go. A sharp kid can get you painted into a corner.

Use as much humor as possible. If you have to choose between boredom and what might be perceived as entertainment — well, I happen to think it's a sin to bore kids in church. The gospel of our Lord Jesus is exciting good news. It can, it should, it must be made so for the kids.

Don't read your story, no matter how well you feel you can. The children are worth the time it takes to memorize it.

So having said all this, I commit these stories to you and your precious children, praying that God's spirit will cement his truth in each of their hearts. And have fun! I always do.

WHAT GOD DOES FOR US

#1
HERE'S A BATTERY THAT LASTS FOREVER

The Holy Spirit's Power

(Have a flashlight small enough to fit in a pocket or purse.)

Guess what I have in my pocket/purse. It sure is handy on a dark night when you're looking for something. It's a flashlight! *(Take it out and shine it toward the children.)* What do flashlights give you? *(Wait)* Light! Of course.

Light is wonderful. Suppose you were in bed one really dark night. You heard a noise, woke up, and it was dark, and you were a little bit scared. *(In hushed voice)* Then the door opened a crack, you saw a hand come in and — *(The following part fast)* it flipped the light switch and the whole room was filled with light. It was your mother. She heard the sound too and came in to see if you were okay. Isn't light wonderful?

Or maybe one day you were playing with your dad's tools and left one in the yard. That evening he was looking for it. *(Loudly)* "Who took my tool without asking me?" "I did," you said. Then he said, "You take a flashlight and you find it!" So you did and you found it! Isn't light wonderful?

Where do we get most of our light? That's right, from the sun. What would happen if the sun stopped shining? We would all freeze! *(Shiver)* All the plants would die, and *we* would all die too.

But what is the light we need more than the sun? Jesus! Jesus said, "I am the light of the world. Whoever walks with me will never walk in darkness." We can do bad things when we walk in darkness, can't we? Jesus wants us to talk in the light, so he gave us his flashlight. *(Hold Bible out, face forward, moving it back and forth as if it might be a flashlight.)* The Bible is God's light, helping us to walk and live the way he wants us to. God puts a battery in our hearts. Now the more I use *this* flashlight *(Show it)*, the weaker the battery gets, but the Holy Spirit is the battery God gave us. The more we use *this* light *(Show Bible)*, the stronger the Holy Spirit battery in our hearts gets, and the better we can see to walk with Jesus.

Psalm 119:105

Your word is a lamp to my feet and a light for my path. *(NIV)*

#2

HEY, I DIDN'T KNOW
I WAS EATING THAT!

The Bitter and the Better

(You should try to determine ahead of time who and how many of the children will cooperate with this. If you anticipate any difficulty, it would be better to find one or two whom you can work with and get from them the assurance that they will taste the things offered and that they will react to them. The stronger their reaction, the more fun it will be.

(Put into small paper cups a portion of the following: Flour, baking soda, salt, sugar, vanilla [possibly diluted a little], shortening, chocolate chips.)

This morning I want you to think of all the things you like to do. You know, like playing ball, or eating (yummy stuff of course), playing dolls, going to Disneyland, watching cartoons. *(Get a significant number.)*

Now, tell me some of the things you don't like to do. Study, go to bed, eat your vegetables, clean up your room, etc. *(Get several expressed.)*

Okay. Now comes the fun part. I'm going to ask some of you to close your eyes, and I'm going to ask you to taste something; and when you do, I want you to tell me if it's good or if it tastes yucky. But nothing I give you will be bad to eat — you have eaten it before. Maybe I will give it only to those who are brave. Anyone who is chicken doesn't have to do it.

Now, who wants to try? *(Have as many of the kids do this as will, but of course you should have each item tasted by at least one child, and a large enough portion of the less pleasant taste to get a reaction.)*

Now before I tell you what you tasted, tell me, would you like it if you only had fun things to do? Things that were easy, things that didn't make you tired, things that tasted good? That it was never too hot, or never too cold? It never rained when you wanted to play outside? That all vegetables tasted like ice cream, and picking up your toys was as much fun as Disneyland?

Why didn't God make things be that way? Doesn't he love us? God does love us, and that's why he doesn't give us all fun, easy things. Because if he did, when we got big, we would be weak, good for nothing.

Now I'm going to tell you what you tasted. There were some that were good; some you didn't like at all, did you? That's what God does with us. He gives us the easy and the hard things. He gives us rain and sun, fun and hard work, happy and sad days, because all together, they make us what he wants us to be.

Now what would happen if you put together all those things you tasted, mixed them up really well, and put it in the oven and baked it? *(Wait) Chocolate Chip Cookies!* That's how chocolate chip cookies are made. Can you make chocolate chip cookies with just the good things? No! You need the yummy and the yucky together.

And God gives us the easy and the hard things because he wants to make something a lot better than chocolate chip cookies.

Matthew 5:45

He causes his sun to rise on the evil and the good, and sends rain on the righteous and the unrighteous. *(NIV)*

#3

BABY IS LOST IN THE SNOW

The Good Shepherd

I am going to tell you a story this morning about a sheep rancher who loved his one hundred sheep so much, he could call each one of them by name. One winter night it was snowing, and he and his wife were just finishing dinner. While she cleared off the table and washed dishes, he went out to the barn to see if everything was all right with the sheep, just as he did every night before locking up. But on that night he stayed out in the barn quite a while, and his wife wondered why. She was rather nervous because she had seen a big wolf on the top of the hill near their ranch that day. But finally he came in, and she asked him, "Why did you stay so long? Is everything all right?" "No," he said, "one of the lambs is missing." "Are you sure?" she asked. "Yes, I counted them three times. Only ninety-nine." "Who was missing?" "Baby," he said. "Oh, no, not Baby again — she is always wandering off. What a terrible night to be lost — all this snow, and the wind blowing so hard, and it's so cold!" The rancher said he wanted to go looking, but it was so dark he could hardly see his hand in front of his face. So there was nothing they could do. They pulled up their chairs in front of the woodstove and tried to read, but all they could do was think about Baby out in the snow. Everytime the wind blew, it sounded just like Baby crying.

Finally, there was nothing to do but go to bed. But he couldn't sleep. Oh, he knew it was just the wind he heard and not Baby crying, but just the same . . . He put the pillow over his head, but it didn't do any good. He knew Baby was out there somewhere. Finally he said, "I can't stand it any longer. I've got to go look. I've got to see if I can find that lamb." "It's too dark, it's too cold. There's too much snow," his wife said. "I know, I know," he said, "but I've got to go."

He pulled some heavy pants on over his pajamas, put on a big parka, tied the hood down tight, pulled on his heavy boots and mittens, and out in the snow he went. He made a circle around the house and barn, then he made another, and another. Each time he got further away. One hour passed, and still no lamb. He rested a minute, then started out again, but he got only a little way when he tripped over a big pile of snow and fell flat on his face. Then he heard a faint cry. He looked down. *(Lots of emotion here.)* That lump of snow — it was *Baby!* "Baby! Baby! Baby!" he cried. He picked up that little lamb, brushed off all the snow, threw her over his shoulder, and headed back to the ranch. And while he walked, he began to sing. *(For added drama, when you say the words "he began to sing," you may have an off-stage voice or the choir sing a song about the shepherd and sheep, such as "The Ninety and Nine," a capella, while you pantomime singing and carrying a lamb.)*

You children know who this story is about, don't you? It's about each one of you. Jesus is our good shepherd. He loves each one of us. He never wants us to run away. He will always try to bring us back, to pick us up. Remember, it was hard for Baby out there in the cold, and it's hard and dangerous when kids don't stay close to our Good Shepherd, Jesus.

John 10:11

I am the good shepherd. The good shepherd lays down his life for the sheep. *(NIV)*

#4

HE CAN BE EVERYWHERE AT THE SAME TIME

God's Omnipresence

Did you ever wish that Jesus had not gone to heaven, that he could be with us here today? So we could see him, talk to him, and he could talk to us? The disciples wanted the same thing. They didn't want Jesus to leave. They wanted him to be with them as they went about teaching and preaching. But Jesus said, "It's good for you if I go away, because when I do, I will send my spirit" (we call him the Holy Spirit), "and he will teach you, he will guide you, he will live in your hearts." You see, Jesus as a man could only be in one place at a time, and every church in America would want him to be in *their* service, so he might not ever get to *ours*.

But the Holy Spirit can be in Alaska, Africa, Colombia, and China, all at the same moment, and it's his job to show people that they need Jesus. He helps us to live for Jesus, tells us what to do, and what not to do, if we ask him. The Bible says it grieves him — that means it makes him sad — if we don't listen to him.

Did you ever notice that if your mom tells you to do something and you don't do it, her voice gets louder and louder every time she says it again? Did you notice that? But do you know what — the Holy Spirit's voice gets softer and softer and softer and softer each time you don't listen. *(Each "softer" should get softer until finally the children just see your lips moving.)* His voice doesn't really get softer — your heart gets harder each time, and you can't hear him.

So if you know God wants you to do something, do it right away, and you will always be able to hear his voice.

John 14:26

But the counselor, the Holy Spirit, whom the Father will send in my name, will teach you all things and will remind you of everything I have said to you. *(NIV)*

#5
YOU DON'T EVEN NEED AN APPOINTMENT

God's Availability

Do you like it when people do things just for you? When somebody says, "I want to take you somewhere, just the two of us." We like to be with other kids, but it's special when it's just for you.

Now suppose you went to *(a large stadium or auditorium the children are familiar with)*, and Jesus was there to speak to everyone. That would be wonderful. But suppose he came to your room to speak just to you. Wouldn't that be great?

Did you know Jesus will do that, talk just to you? Did you know the Bible was written just for you? You can pick it up, read it, and know Jesus is speaking to you. You and Jesus have a date. You sure wouldn't want to miss that, would you?

Now suppose you wanted to talk to some very important person, maybe the principal of your school, or the mayor of your town, or the governor, or even our president. Well, you would have to make an appointment. They might say, "He can see you for five minutes next month at 2 o'clock."

But Jesus, the King of Kings, the Lord of Lords — you can talk to him anytime! You never need an appointment.

Psalm 116:1, 2

I love the Lord, for he heard my voice; he heard my cry for mercy. Because he turned his ear to me, I will call on him as long as I live. *(NIV)*

#6

IT'S NOT FAIR

He Took Our Place

Let's pretend again this morning. Let's pretend you are all in the same class at school. You are supposed to be studying, but somebody is whispering and the teacher hears. They always hear, don't they? She says, "You know I said I don't want any whispering, so now you are all going to have to stay in at recess and write 50 times: "I won't whisper in class."

If you were not the one who was whispering, what would you say? "It's not fair. That's not right; I shouldn't be punished for somebody else." That *wouldn't* be fair, would it? Does it ever happen?

Now suppose everybody in the class was misbehaving but you. You were the only one who was behaving well, but the teacher punished you and not them. That would *really* not be fair, would it?

Now suppose this happened again — everybody else was bad. But you were good, and again the teacher punished you, and they all got to go out and play, and do you know what else? When they got outside they looked in the window and made fun of you. "Ya-ya-ya-ya-ya-ya, you got just what you deserved, ha ha ha! It serves you right. You thought you were so good!"

Boy, how would you feel then? Do you think that ever happened? That a person who never did anything bad was punished, and all the bad people weren't punished at all? Yes, that's what happened to Jesus. He was the only good person who ever lived, the only one who never sinned, yet he was crucified in place of all the bad people who ever lived, and do you know what else? When he was dying, hurting so bad, the people laughed at him. But did he get mad? No, he said, "Father, forgive them because they don't know what they are doing." Did you know that crucifixion was the cruelest, the most horrible punishment anyone could ever have?

Now if you were to ask Jesus why he let them do that to him, do you know what I think he would say? "I had to die in that horrible way because I'm taking the place of the worst man, the cruelest criminals that ever lived. And if he will confess and is truly sorry and accept me as his Lord and Savior, he can come to heaven with me." Jesus died for people just like that and for people like you and me.

Isaiah 53:5

But he was pierced for our transgressions, he was crushed for our iniquities; the punishment that brought us peace was upon him, and by his wounds we are healed. *(NIV)*

#7

LIFE COMES OUT OF DEATH — IT'S TRUE

A New Beginning

I want to tell you a story about a five-year-old girl who lived on a sheep ranch with her mommy and daddy. She loved being in kindergarten, but at this time of year she couldn't wait to get home because this was lambing time. This was the time the new lambs were born, and she liked to help her daddy in the barn. Just as a doctor helped your mommy when you were born, her daddy helped the sheep when the lambs were born.

One day as she was getting off the bus from school, she heard a cry from the barn. She knew what that meant. One of the sheep was going to have a baby lamb, but she knew the sheep was hurting really bad because of the way it was crying. She ran to the barn, calling her daddy, but he wasn't there. As soon as she got there, she could see the lamb was being born. But the mama sheep was stuck between two posts, and she looked as if she was going to die. The little girl tried to do everything she had watched her daddy do, and in just a few minutes the lamb was there. But the mother lived for only a few hours. The wooly little baby lamb lived. The mother died. You see, life came out of death. This may be hard for you to understand, but almost all life comes out of death. Something has to die before something can be born.

Let me show you what I mean. Suppose your mom saw a beautiful bush in your neighbor's garden, and the neighbor said, "Here's a seed. If you plant this, you'll get a bush just like mine." So she did, and the bush grew to be just as beautiful. You wanted to surprise your mom, and so you decided to dig down, get the seed and plant it someplace else so she could have two bushes. You did this, but all you found was two little hard skins. The seed died, and out of it came the beautiful plant. You see — life out of death.

Or maybe one of you started to take piano lessons, and

your teacher said, "I think you could be a fine pianist some day — even a concert pianist." You'd like that. But then she said, "But you would have to practice two hours a day after school." So what would have to die before the pianist could be born? Some of your play time.

You see, again, life out of death. God wanted us to have a chance to be in heaven with him. But we were too bad, and we'd spoil heaven. So he found a way. He sent his son Jesus to die for our sins so that we could be forgiven, so we could have eternal life. We got life from Jesus' death — life out of death. Isn't God good?

John 3:16

For God so loved the world that he gave his one and only Son, that whoever believes in him shall not perish but have eternal life. *(NIV)*

#8

LOOK HOW BEAUTIFUL I AM!

God Made Us Special

Do you kids like birds? There are so many different kinds, aren't there? Some big, some little, some very beautiful, and some, well, are just birds, and nobody would think they were special at all. If you were to ask people what they think is the most beautiful bird of all, they would probably say it's the peacock. It's a big bird, and it's a very proud bird. When it walks around, it looks as though it is sticking its nose up in the air and saying, "Look at me. Look how beautiful I am."

I'm going to tell you a bird story this morning, and it's about a peacock and some of his friends. They were all gathered in a big tree in the forest, and the peacock was complaining. "People say I'm beautiful, and I know I am. But when I start to sing, everybody covers their ears." It's true that the peacock makes a horrible sound when it sings. "Why can't I have a beautiful voice too? I want to sing like other birds," it said. Well, one of the other birds was a big, brown, ugly buzzard, and he said to the peacock, "Well, at least you're beautiful. Look at me. Everybody thinks I'm ugly. I don't know why I can't have beautiful feathers. It's not fair." Then the dove spoke up, "Well, Mr. Buzzard, at least you're brave. I wish I was. You're not afraid of anything. I'm afraid of everything. It's awful." Just then the pheasant came up and said to the dove, "At least people are not always hunting you. I can fly fast and I've got pretty feathers, but I have to watch out every minute, or else I'll get shot. I wish I were somebody else." "I do too," said the other birds.

Just then a sparrow flew into the tree. He was singing and chirping. He knew he was not very pretty, but he didn't care. "What are you so happy about?" the other birds wanted to know. "There's surely nothing special about you. You're not big, you're not brave, you're not a good fighter, you're not pretty, you're nothing!"

"That's all right," said the sparrow, "I'm just the way God made me, and that's just fine. That's all I want to be — just the way God made me."

Then you know what he did? He just flew off whistling happily while all the other birds sat there grumping and wishing they were like somebody else. *(At this point, when we told this story we asked one of the ladies in the audience to sing one verse and chorus of "His Eye Is on the Sparrow." She sang this without accompaniment from where she sat. This, of course, was prearranged.)*

You know, kids, that's why so many people are unhappy all the time. They always wish they were like somebody else instead of the way God made them.

God knew what he was doing when he made each one of you. He made you just the way he wanted you to be, and he made you special.

Philippians 4:12

I know what it is to be in need, and I know what it is to have plenty. I have learned the secret of being content in any and every situation, whether well fed or hungry, whether living in plenty or in want. *(NIV)*

#9

LET 'EM IN — THEY'RE WITH ME!

Knowing Jesus

Do you kids like to go to parties? What is the most fun about them — games or refreshments? Well, I'm going to tell you about the most wonderful party that ever was.

A great king sent out an invitation: "Everyone is invited to my party," he said. "I don't want anyone to be missing, because I love all my people." Well, the people were very excited about that, especially the poor people. Nobody ever invited them to parties, so they started for the palace. But before they got to the door, some people said, "You can't go in, you've only been to the fourth grade in school. To others they said, "Look at you, your clothes are worn out; you don't even look as though you took a bath today. You can't go to this party. What can you do? You can't sing, you can't play, you don't have any money. Nobody cares about you. You're not pretty, you're not handsome, you'd better go home."

Well, the poor people knew this was true, but all the same, they were very sad, and they started to go home. But just then the prince walked up. He heard what those people said, and do you know what he said? He said, "They're with me!"

Well, let me tell you, those palace gates swung wide open and all those poor people walked right in. And do you know what else? As soon as they got into that palace, their ragged clothes turned to beautiful robes.

Now tell me, who was the prince? Who was the king? What was the palace? This is a story about Jesus, isn't it? He was the prince. And it's true, you don't have to be anybody special to go to heaven with Jesus. You just have to know him and love him, and he will say, "They're with me!"

Matthew 22:9, 10

Go to the street corners and invite to the banquet anyone you find. So the servants went out into the streets and gathered all the people they could find, both good and bad, and the wedding hall was filled with guests. *(NIV)*

#10
LOOK WHO CAME TO LIVE IN MY TREE
Give God Your Heart

Do you know what somebody built in my yard? A house! That's right. Somebody I don't even know built a house in my yard to raise a family in. This is true. They built it in one of my trees, and I didn't even see them do it. And do you know who lives in it? A family of birds.

It was a beautiful house made of little sticks. How do you suppose they did it? Did they just fly to a bunch of twigs, pull some out, then go drop them on a branch? Oh, no! That would never hold the eggs, and the first wind would blow it off. No, they have to build the nest very carefully, one stick at a time. They tuck them in and out *(Demonstrate)* so it will be really strong.

When all the sticks are in place, it will still be too rough for their babies, so they bring up a lot of fine grass, bits of string, and little pieces of cloth to make it warm and soft. Once a lady who lives in Arcadia, California, washed some nylon stockings and hung them on a chair to dry in the sun. A big crow swooped down, picked up one of those stockings, and carried it to the nest she was building way up on the top of a tall tree. I think they must have very fashionable crows in Arcadia. *(This happened to the author's neighbor. The nest was in the author's tall Eucalyptus tree.)*

Just think what they can do, just using their feet and beaks. How did they learn to do that? Who showed them how? God did, didn't he?

Say, I just thought of something. Do you kids realize each of you is building a nest? *(Wait)* You don't think so? Yes, you are, even though you don't have beaks and feathers. Yes, you are building your life nest. You are building the life you are going to have to live in. That bird in my yard built a good nest. But if he had built a bad one, then that's what he would have to live in.

How do you build a good life nest? A life's nest that will

be good when you are big? You can't wait till then; you've got to start now. That crow didn't wait until winter, when it was snowing and the wind was blowing. So what can you do now? Well, every good house has a good foundation. My bird's house had heavy twigs for its foundation. God gives us one in the Bible. It says, "Son . . . daughter . . . give me your heart." When you give God your heart, you have a perfect start for building your life's nest. You will be able to understand the plans or the blueprints that God has put in the Bible. You'll know where to go, know whom to talk to when you have trouble.

You see, God told that crow, just as he tells all the animals, how to live and behave. He will tell us, too, if we ask.

Proverbs 23:26

My son, give me your heart and let your eyes keep to my ways. *(NIV)*

WHAT WE DO
FOR GOD

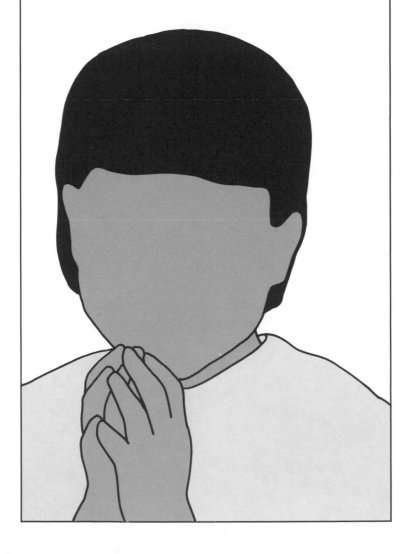

#11
WHAT A LAZY BUNCH OF PEOPLE!

Doing Our Part

There was once a king who saw that he had a lot of lazy people in his kingdom. It seemed as though they were always waiting for somebody else to do the things that needed to be done. Now the king loved his people, and he did not want to punish them, but he really wanted them to be different — to always do their part. He decided on a good way to teach them a lesson.

There was a road that ran in front of the castle, and most of the people in that village passed down it every day. So one dark night the king sent two of his trusted servants out with a shovel, a large rock, and a box in which the king put a real treasure. They dug a deep hole in the road, put in the treasure box, and on top of the box, they put the rock. Just the top of the rock stuck out, enough so that every time the people rode their carts over it, the wheels went *bump* and really shook them up. The people would say, "I wonder why somebody doesn't dig out that rock." "Why doesn't the king get somebody to do it?"

One day a young man came along and saw that rock and thought, "You know, that shouldn't be there. Somebody's cart could get broken, or they might get such a hard bump they could turn over." So he went home and got a shovel, and he dug out the rock. Now what do you suppose he found underneath? Right! The treasure! Did this really happen? Is this a true story? No, it's just made up. But it surely tells us something that *is* true.

We could wish we were really strong. We might pray and ask God to give us strong bodies so we could be good at sports, but do we eat the way we should? Do we get the exercise we should?

We might pray, "Dear Jesus, please help me get good grades in school." But maybe we don't want to study or do our homework. God is not going to reward us if we are lazy or disobedient. But if we see a job that's hard to do, and we go ahead and do it, then all through our life God will be rewarding us. And it will be a lot better than any buried treasure.

Proverbs 19:15

Laziness brings on deep sleep, and the shiftless man goes hungry. *(NIV)*

#12

LET'S CHOOSE UP SIDES
Making Good Choices

Do you kids like to choose? You know, like when you play baseball? You choose the team you will be on. I choose Matt — I choose Charlie — Sally — I want to be on your side, choose me. *(Say this as kids would.)* Or when you go to a restaurant you choose to just have dessert, but your mom chooses something else for you. Or maybe you go to a potluck and there are so many things to choose, you can't decide which. When you're in Sunday school the superintendent says, "What song shall we sing?" So you choose.

Did you know you choose lots of times a day? When you get up in the morning, you choose. You can be real grumpy — "I don't want to get up, I'm still sleepy." "I don't want that for breakfast" — "I don't want to wear that dress." You can choose to be like that, or you can jump out of bed and say, "Hi, Mom, what's for breakfast?" "I can't wait to go to school!" You can choose to be like that.

When you get to school you can choose to study and listen and learn, do your homework and get a good education; or you can choose to not study, not do your homework, and grow up to be a dummy. You can choose.

You can choose to not follow Jesus, but that would be such a *bad* choice. I'm going to tell you a story about two people in the Bible and the choices they made. One was Peter and the other was Demas. Peter made a bad choice when he chose to tell someone he didn't know Jesus. Oh, how sorry he was later. After Jesus rose from the dead, he told Peter that he was going to be treated just the way Jesus was. But that didn't stop Peter. He chose to follow Jesus, no matter what. Now almost 2,000 years later, when we think about Peter, we think what a wonderful apostle he was. But not Demas. He was one of the disciples too. He thought following Jesus was too hard. He deserted Paul. He was a quitter. That's what you think of when you hear his name.

So whenever you choose up sides for anything, think of this story. Remember, God wants you to be on his side, his team. If you're on God's team, you'll be a winner!

Philippians 4:13

I can do everything through him who gives me strength. *(NIV)*

#13
WATCH OUT FOR THE BIG BULLDOZER!
Building Godly Lives

Do you kids like to build things? Did you ever build a little house out of sticks in your yard, or maybe with Lego blocks? Did you ever watch a carpenter build a real house? What do they do first? They put in the foundation, don't they? That's important; it's got to be strong and straight. Hey, you know *(As if coming up with a new idea)*, it's like boys and girls. Good foods, lots of sleep, studying hard at school, playing hard at home, learning about Jesus — that's a good foundation for any kid.

Well, next come the walls of the house. They are for protection. They keep all the good things in and the bad things out. Your mom, your dad and your Sunday school teacher try to put nothing but good things in your mind and heart, and keep the bad things out.

But do you know what protects you the most? The roof. It covers us whenever we are inside and under it. But it can't cover us when we go out, can it?

It's sort of like God's love and protection — it will cover us as long as we want it to, but if we disobey God, disobey our mom and dad, and if we want our own way no matter what, then we are not under God's roof, and some bad things can happen.

How long does it take to build a house like the one you live in? Many months to build a good one. Do you know how long it takes to tear one down? They can do it in *one day*. A big ugly bulldozer smashes it. They pick up the pieces in a big scoop, put it in a big truck, and haul it to the dump. They could do this with a beautiful new house.

Say, I just thought of something. Did you know you carry your house around with you all day? Yes, you do. It's with you wherever you go. *(Point to head, body and limbs.)* This is your real house; the real you lives inside.

God wants you to protect your house. He will help you

if you let him. But remember, there is somebody who doesn't love you, and he has a big bulldozer and you know who that is.

But he can't touch you unless *you let him.*

Matthew 7:24

Therefore everyone who hears these words of mine and puts them into practice is like a wise man who built his house on the rock. *(NIV)*

#14
WHO REALLY GAVE THE MOST MONEY?
Stewardship

(For this story you will need three hats, each sufficiently different from the others so that the children will identify the three characters by them. You should have a dress hat, a sports hat, and a knit hat, one that can be pulled down over the ears. Have knit hat in pocket, and place sports hat where it can be picked up some distance from where you are standing. The dress hat should be on the opposite side. You will need an aluminum pie tin and some fifty pennies. In one pocket put two pennies; in another, eight; and in another, forty. Arrange ahead of time to have one of the children help you. She will hold the pie tin, and when you pass by she will say: "Please sir, will you help our Sunday school mission project?" This you will do three times, each time wearing one of the hats.)

Good morning, kids. We are going to have a pretend story this morning. Let's pretend that *(Child's name)* is standing in front of our church with an offering plate, asking people to give to our mission project *(Or whatever)*.

(Have child stand in place, and you then put on the knit hat, pulled down over your ears; turn your collar up, and walk slowly in a slightly stooped manner, as would an aged person. When you reach where she is standing, she asks:) "Please, sir, will you help our Sunday school mission project?" *(You reply in an old and tired voice:)* "I'll do what I can; I wish it were more." *(You drop in two pennies, one at a time, so they can be heard. You then walk to where you have placed the sports hat [still in character], remove knit hat, turn collar down, put on sports hat, and return to girl. She repeats the same request. You reply in a very lighthearted way:)* "Oh, sure, always happy to help out a worthy cause." *(You drop in eight pennies, one at a time.)*

(Go to where you have placed dress hat, remove sports hat, and with dress hat now on, you return to child. She

repeats same question. You say in a very pompous tone:) "Oh, certainly. I enjoy giving. I give a lot." *(Make show of dropping in 20 or so pennies. Remove hat and have child sit.)*

Now, children, which one gave the most money? *(Point to or hold up the various hats.)* You think this one did *(Holding up dress hat)*? Is that what you all think? Oh, no! The Bible says he gave the least. Look how much he had left. *(Show twenty pennies not given. Now put on knit hat, turn up collar.)* The Bible says that this man gave the most, even though it was only two pennies. Look *(Show empty pocket)*, he put in all he had.

You see, kids, God does not look at how much we give; he looks at how much we have left, how much we could have given.

So when you have your own money to give to Jesus, give as much as you can, and God will say, "It's a lot."

Mark 12:43, 44

Calling his disciples to him, Jesus said, "I tell you the truth, this poor widow has put more into the treasury than all the others. They all gave out of their wealth; but she, out of her poverty, put in everything — all she had to live on." *(NIV)*

#15

HEY, THAT BIRD'S TALKING

Praising God

Have any of you children ever had a parrot or parakeet? *(If yes)* Did you ever try to teach it to talk? Some parakeets can say twenty to thirty words, and even sentences.

I heard about a family that tried to get their bird to say, "Praise the Lord." *(This was the author's family.)* But do you know what he said? He said, "Praise the birdie." But suppose he did learn to say, "Praise the Lord." Would he know what he was saying? No, he would just be repeating words. But is it possible for a parakeet to really praise the Lord? You don't think so? Oh, yes, it can. The Bible says so. God's word says, "Let everything that has breath praise the Lord."

But how does a parakeet praise the Lord? *(Wait)* Just by doing and being what God created him to do and be. Now, how can boys and girls praise the Lord? To say it ten times a day, morning, noon, and night? That's fine, but let me tell you another way.

The Bible says, "Children, obey your parents in the Lord." When you do that, you're praising the Lord. The Bible says, "Love one another, as I have loved you." When you do that, you're praising the Lord.

Every time you do what God wants you to do — when you do what pleases our Lord Jesus — you're really praising the Lord, and not just repeating words, like that parakeet.

Psalm 61:8

Then will I ever sing praise to your name and fulfill my vows day after day. *(NIV)*

#16
DON'T FORGET WHO YOU REALLY ARE
Reflecting Jesus

Does your mom ever leave you notes — you know, reminders? Maybe a note on the refrigerator door that says, "Don't touch the dessert." Or she puts one in your lunchbox, tucked in with your chocolate chip cookies so you'll be sure to see it. It says, "Be sure you bring home your workbook."

Do we all need reminders? I know I surely do. Did you know God told us to do this? He says we should write ourselves notes to remember how good he has been to us, and how we should serve him. Where should we write them? On the refrigerator door, or on the bathroom mirror? God told the children of Israel to write them on the door posts and on their gates. That's so they would see them many times a day.

If you put one on your gate, what would be a good thing for it to say? "Don't let the dog out." You know, I can think of a good sign for your gate so you would see it everytime you went anywhere. How about this one: "Remember who you are." Does that sound kind of dumb? You don't think you could ever forget who you are? Oh, yes you can.

There's a preacher whose dad always said that when his son left the house for the day or for the evening. He said, "Remember who you are." He meant, remember who your father is. Remember how it would hurt us if you did something bad. Remember, your real name is Christian — that's who you really are.

Or the sign could say, "Remember, you are God's ambassador." Do you know what an ambassador is? Our government sends a person to every big country. If someone wants to know something about our country, he asks the ambassador. When he sees him and talks to him, he is seeing and talking to us.

So we are God's ambassadors. If anybody wants to know what Jesus said, they can talk to us. If they want to know what Jesus is like, they can look at us. So we surely want to be good ambassadors.

Philemon 1:6

I pray that you may be active in sharing your faith, so that you will have a full understanding of every good thing we have in Christ. *(NIV)*

#17

I BETCHA I'M STRONGER THAN YOU ARE

Prayer

I'm going to tell you a story that perhaps your mom has read to you sometime. It's about a big argument between two very strong people. But in a hundred years you could never guess who these people are. One said, "I'm stronger than you are." The other said, "No, you're not — I am." "You're not either — I am, and I can prove it." "Okay, you try." Do you know who these people were? It was the sun and the wind arguing. This is, of course, a pretend story.

So the wind said, "You see that man coming? Let's see who can make him take his coat off." The sun said, "Okay, you go first. The one who can do it will be the strongest." So the wind blew a tremendous blast. It knocked all the buttons off the man's coat. They went flying. But the man just pulled his coat around tighter and walked on. Then the wind blew another blast, even harder than the one before. This time it knocked the man over and tore his coat, but he was still wearing it. "Well," the wind said, "just watch this one." Again he blew, and it was almost like a tornado. The man rolled over and over down the path like a big ball. His coat ripped right up the back, but he held it closer, and on he went. "It's your turn, Mr. Sun — I give up," said the wind.

"Well," Mr. Sun said, "that man really likes wearing his coat. He doesn't want to take it off. I'm going to have to find a way to make him want to take it off." So the sun just gave the man a big, warm smile. Then a warmer one. Then a warmer one even than that. Pretty soon the man said, "Boy, it's getting to be a nice warm day. I think I'll take off my coat." And so he did, and the sun won.

Now why did I tell you this story? It's really a wonderful story about prayer. You don't think so? Well, let me show you. Suppose you have a friend who is always doing something you know she shouldn't. But whenever you tell her about it, she gets mad. The more you tell her she should quit, the more she wants to do it. So you decide you won't mention it anymore. You will just ask Jesus to tell her. Every time you think about it, you ask Jesus to show her, and then Jesus just shines down on her with his love. God's Son puts it in her heart not to want to do that thing she shouldn't, and you notice that she doesn't do it anymore. See, that's how prayer works.

Whenever you've got a problem, talk first to Jesus about it. He knows the best way to do things.

I Peter 5:7

Cast all your anxiety on him because he cares for you. *(NIV)*

#18

WATCH OUT — IT MIGHT POP!
Freedom to Do Right

(Get a large balloon. Blow it up ahead of time to deter-mine how large you can without its breaking. As you tell the story, blow it up in stages. Let the air out at appropriate times.)

You kids don't remember, of course, but when you were babies, your world was pretty small. There wasn't any place you could go on your own; you had to be carried. By yourself, you could only roll over to the sides of your crib. *(Blow balloon up a bit.)* When you got a little older and learned to crawl, your world got bigger *(Another blow)* and you went all around the house. Next you learned to walk; then you had more freedom. *(Blow balloon.)* You walked around the yard. Boy, you thought you were big. But you still had to stay in the yard until you could be trusted to go out. Then later you could *(Blow balloon)* go across the street to play with the other kids. Your mom told you about watching for cars, and never to get into a car with anyone you didn't know, and how to behave at somebody else's house. If you did what she said, she let you have more freedom. *(Blow balloon.)* But if you didn't, back into the yard you came. *(Let some air out.)* "Okay, because you didn't mind me, you've got to stay in the yard for the rest of the day." Did your mom ever say that? Then you had to start all over again to show her you could be trusted.

Did you ever wish your mom would let you do anything you wanted? Well, do you know what happens when moms and dads don't really love their kids? They let them do any-thing they want, see anything they want, and read anything they want. I'll show you — watch. They get all the freedom they want. *(Blow balloon until it breaks, or pop it with a pin, but only after you have blown it up considerably more. Hold up broken balloon.)* This doesn't look like much fun, does it? But that's what happens when we want to do what Jesus says we shouldn't. Do you think Jesus wants you to have fun? Sure he does. He wants you to grow up to be a wonderfully happy Christian. Now I'm going to tell you a secret, and you may not believe me, but it's true — and this is going to surprise you. As you get bigger and really learn to love and follow Jesus, he will open the whole world to you. You can do anything you want to. That's what I said, *anything* you want to! And do you know why? Because anyone who really loves Jesus will only want to do what will make Jesus happy. So if you want to do something, Jesus will say, "Sure, go ahead, do it." Boy, doesn't that make you want to love Jesus more and more?

Galatians 5:13

You, my brothers, were called to be free. But do not use your freedom to indulge the sinful nature; rather, serve one another in love. *(NIV)*

#19
THAT'S WHAT I GAVE YOU EARS FOR
Listening to the Lord

Let's suppose this morning. Let's suppose that when you sat down for breakfast, your mom gave you a bowl, a spoon, and a box of Cheerios. She filled the bowl with Cheerios, and then poured in the milk. Oh, and she put down a plastic table mat because you sometimes spill a little. So you begin to eat. *(Go through motions. Take fingers and reach into the bowl. Take some Cheerios and eat them. Pick up the bowl and drink some milk. Reach into the bowl again with fingers and take more Cheerios and eat them. For a little comedy, after each mouthful, shake fingers as though shaking off milk, and wipe fingers on sleeve. If you don't want that much comedy, show wiping hands on napkin.)*

Now if your mom saw you do that, what would she say? *"Use your spoon!* That's why I gave it to you. That's what spoons are for."

Or let's pretend your dad sent you out to rake leaves. He gave you a leaf rake and a trash can to put the leaves in. So you took your foot and pushed the leaves into little piles. *(Illustrate)* Then you picked them up with your hands and put them in the trash can.

Now if your Dad saw you do that, what would he say? "Use the rake. That's why I gave it to you. That's what rakes are made for."

Would we ever do things like that? *(Wait)* I think we do it every day. Does your mom ever tell you to do something, but you're not listening? Do you know what I think God would say about that? "I gave you ears. Listen to your mom. That's what ears are for." Do you not see some of the things you should do? I'm always leaving my clothes around the house for my wife to pick up. *(Substitute something that applies to you.)* What do you think God would say to me? "Don't you *see* how messy it looks? Don't you see it makes your wife unhappy? I gave you eyes. Use them. That's why I *gave* them to you."

Are there times we should be reading our Bible, but we don't? Do you know what I think God would say about that? "Read your Bible! My Son's story is in it! That's why I gave it to you."

Did you ever do anything you knew was wrong, but you didn't tell Jesus you were sorry and ask him to forgive you? What would God say about that? I think he'd say, "Don't you believe me? Tell me every bad thing that you do. Tell me you're sorry. My Son Jesus died on the cross so that I can forgive you."

Now we know why God gave us ears, eyes, mind, and heart. He wants us to *use them* — doesn't he?

I Samuel 3:9

". . . Speak, Lord, for your servant is listening."

WHAT WE DO
FOR OTHERS

#20
WHEN DID I DO THAT, JESUS?
Helping Others

This morning I'm going to tell you a parable. It's a made-up story, but it's absolutely true. It's sort of like the parables that Jesus told.

One day there was a little boy who wanted very much to go down to the Sea of Galilee to see Jesus. His pals said Jesus was down there, and he was healing people. The boy's pals were outside calling him, and he started to go out when his mom said, "Samuel, before you go, will you go over to our neighbor Joseph's house? He's been sick, and I'm worried about him. See if he is okay. See if he needs anything. It will only take a minute. Your friends will wait."

But they didn't want to wait, so Samuel said, "I'll catch up with you." Samuel ran quickly to Joseph's house, but Joseph needed a lot of help, and it was fifteen minutes before Samuel could go home and tell his mom that Joseph was okay. His mom thanked him and said, "On your way, will you take this food to Sarah's house? I know she won't have anything to eat tonight if we don't help her." So Samuel said, "Okay, Mom." When he got to Sarah's, she was so happy, but she told Samuel that she had just fallen down and hurt her right arm really bad. Could he help her eat? He said, "Sure."

When he was done, he ran as fast as he could to the water, but he got just a little way when an old man came along looking very sad. He looked as if he was lost. Samuel knew he didn't live in their village. "Can you help me?" the man asked. "I need to find my cousin Jacob — he's the tent maker." "Oh, I know where he lives," Samuel said. "It's over there; I'll show you." So he took him to where he could see Jacob's house.

Then he ran just as fast as he could to the water. But he got only a block or two when he saw his pals coming back. They said, "Boy, you sure missed it. *(Voice of awe.)* We saw

Jesus do something you wouldn't believe!" Well, Samuel went home. He was very sad. He didn't want his mom to know, so he went out in the barn with the goats. He wanted to cry, but he thought he was too big to cry. Then he heard a voice. *(Voice speaks.)* "Samuel, listen to me . . ." *(For the best effect, voice should come over the church's public address system, the one speaking the words not in evidence.)* Somehow he knew it was Jesus. Jesus said: *(Voice speaks)* "I was sick, and you helped me; I was lost, and you showed me the way." Samuel could hardly believe what he was hearing, and he said, "Jesus, when did I do that?" "When you did it for those three needy people that I love, you did it for me," Jesus said. Samuel surely didn't feel like crying anymore.

Would you like to do something for Jesus? You can, just as Samuel did. You find some people who really need help, and help them. Do it for Jesus. You may not hear Jesus' voice, but you can read his words in the Bible that are saying just the same thing, just for you.

I Peter 3:8

Finally, all of you, live in harmony with one another; be sympathetic, love as brothers, be compassionate and humble. *(NIV)*

#21

I CAN'T SEE YOU WITH THIS HAT ON

Putting Others First

(For this story you will need a hat with a fairly stiff crown, some fairly rigid wire, and a small mirror, about 4" x 6". Bend wire around hat band and have one end projecting out in front some eight inches. Secure the mirror to the wire's end so that it hangs in front of the storyteller's eyes, mirror side away from the children. This should be put into a box or bag.)

All you children look well dressed today. Did you dress yourself, or did your mom do it? I've got a riddle for you this morning. What do you wear sometimes that your mom did not put on you, and that you probably don't even know you're wearing? That's a hard one, isn't it? Well, I'll tell you — or maybe I'd better show you, or you wouldn't believe me. This is going to surprise you. First, close your eyes and don't open them until I tell you. All eyes closed? No peeking! *(Put on hat.)* Okay, now open! Now what in the world is this I'm wearing? Did you ever see anyone wear a hat like this? No? Oh, yes, you did; everyone wears one sometime.

This is an I-can-only-see-myself hat. When I'm wearing this I can only see myself, because I'm looking into a mirror. *(Turn mirror to show the children.)*

When you are playing games wearing this hat, you can't see that your friends want a turn too, that they want to play what they want to play for awhile. You can only see yourself — what you want, what you like to do.

You can't see that your mom is tired and she wishes you would clean up your room and put away your toys. You can't see her. With this hat on you can only see yourself.

God says in the Bible that we shouldn't just see ourselves — what we need, what we want. God wants us to see what somebody else needs first. If we don't, if we are always just putting ourselves first, then we're wearing a hat just like this, even though we can't see it.

We all like people to like us, don't we? To want to be with us and play with us? I'll tell you a real secret that will make everybody like you. Don't ever wear this hat. Let other kids go first. Try to help them instead of helping yourself. That's Jesus' way.

(Open your Bible and start to read, but hold it in such a way that the mirror obstructs your view.)

When I'm wearing this hat I can't read my Bible very well. All I can see is myself, what I want — not what God wants to tell me.

Do you know what? I'm going to take off this hat, and you will like me better — and I know Jesus will be happier.

I Corinthians 10:24

Nobody should seek his own good, but the good of others. *(NIV)*

#22

LET'S ALL PLANT A SEED

Planting God's Love

(This story should be made personal by using names of people in the congregation and/or missionaries the children might be familiar with. This would be a good chance to honor a teacher or teachers in general.)

Did you kids ever read the story of Johnny Appleseed? Johnny Appleseed liked apples — they were his favorite food, and he wanted everybody to like them too. So everywhere he went, he planted apple seeds.

Now of course not all of the seeds became trees. Some didn't get enough water, some were planted where there were too many rocks, and some probably got trampled — I think by small boys and girls. *(Give a knowing look.)* But all over the country, apple trees grew because of the seeds he planted.

Did you know we have some Johnny Appleseeds in our church? We sure do. Our Sunday school teachers have been planting God's word, little seeds of faith, in children's hearts for many years. Now some of the children never learned to love Jesus. Some didn't want to listen in Sunday school. Some only came once in awhile, so Jesus never got to feed them God's word from the Bible. But many will be in heaven because of the seeds their teachers planted in little kids' hearts.

All over the world our missionaries are planting the Good News in people's hearts; and all over the world there are churches where there were none before.

Can little kids plant seeds like this? Sure! When people can tell you love Jesus, you're planting a seed.

Galatians 6:9

Let us not become weary in doing good, for at the proper time we will reap a harvest if we do not give up. *(NIV)*

#23

LOOK — MY HANDS CAN SAY I LOVE YOU!

Service

(Storyteller should have one hand in pocket as he faces children.)

Well, kids, I've got something in my hand, and you'll never guess what it is — not in a thousand years. *(Peek into closed hand and smile — little touches like this help to create interest. Respond appropriately to any guesses made.)*

Just as I thought. You couldn't guess. *(Child's name)*, I want you to count to three, and on the count of three I'm going to open my hand. *(On the count of three, hold hand high and open, revealing it to be empty.)* So what did I have in my hand? Nothing? It is empty? Oh, no! My hand is full, and yours is too. Your hands and my hands are full of power — power to do a lot of wonderful things.

Do you know your hand can say I love you? It can say I love you in a thousand ways.

You look as though you don't believe me. Well, I'll show you. Suppose your mommy is very tired, and your toys are scattered all around the house. *(Lots of action with your hands.)* So you go around the house, and as you pick up each toy, your hand is saying, "I love you, Mommy." *(Teller could act as though picking up toys, and with each one say, "I love you.")*

Some missionaries are not allowed to preach or teach about Jesus in the country where they have gone, so they find ways to help people just using their hands. Their hands are saying, "Jesus loves you."

Do you like to hear *(your pianist or organist)* play? Just using his/her fingers, he/she tells about God's love.

Remember, every time you do something with your hands that God wants you to do, your hands are saying "I love you, Jesus."

Now tomorrow is Monday, and you'll be going to school. You have a lot of things to do in the morning, don't you? Can I give you one more thing? A real good thing? Just before you go out the door, hold your hands high and say, "Lord Jesus, help my hands to say 'I love you' today."

Deuteronomy 16:15

For the Lord your God will bless you in all your harvest and in all the work of your hands, and your joy will be complete. *(NIV)*

#24

WE CAN TALK ABOUT ANYBODY— ANYTIME!

Truth With Love

(Storyteller should whisper something in one of the children's ears. Not actual words, but just very audible whisper sounds.)

Now, don't tell anybody what I said. It's just a secret between you and me, and nobody must ever know. *(Teller should smile very smugly and say:)* We have a secret and only *(Child's name)* and I know it, or ever will. *(To [Child's name])*Remember now, don't tell *anybody. (Pause, look as though thinking.)* But you know, it was *not* a secret between just *(Child's name)* and me. Somebody *else* heard it, even though I whispered. Now who do you think it was? Who else knows? *(Wait)* That's right. Jesus knows.

Did you know, the Bible says that one day I may have to stand before God and tell him why I said the things I did? I'm surely glad I didn't say anything bad. But suppose I did. Suppose I said something that was mean or was not true. I'd surely be ashamed to have God hear *that.*

Would you like to be able to say anything you wanted to about anybody, anytime? You can. Just be sure it's *true,* and be sure it's *kind.* Now suppose I had a big red nose. Suppose you said, "Boy, *(Teller's name)* surely has a big red nose. Wow!" Would that be true? Yes, if I did. But it surely wouldn't be kind, would it? Jesus wants us to always tell the truth, and always be loving. If we do that, we can talk about anybody, anytime.

Ephesians 4:25

Therefore each of you must put off falsehood and speak truthfully to his neighbor, for we are all members of one body. *(NIV)*

#25
JUST LIKE KIDS — ALWAYS MOVING
Sharing

(Provide a mobile and a box large enough so that it can be lowered in without tangling — hold box up for children to see.)

Now who can guess what I've got in this box? I'll give a couple of clues. Two hints that will help you guess. The things in this box are kind of like little kids. They are always moving, and they bump sometimes, and if they don't behave, they get all tangled. Can anybody guess? Well, I guess I'll have to show you. *(Slowly lift mobile from box and let it move around.)*

See, it's a mobile — it's always moving. Yet if it doesn't act right, these parts will bump each other. It's kind of like Jesus' family. When we love each other, then everybody gets a chance to sail. *(If mobile is not moving, you might blow on it.)* But suppose one said, "I don't always want to be on top." Another said, "I want to go faster." *(Change voice sound with each.)* "No, it's too fast already . . ." "I'm not going to play anymore . . ." "You're not fair . . ." "You're cheating." *(These should be said in a child's argumentative tone.)* Do you know what would happen? *Nobody* would have any fun. Everybody would be mad and tangled. Jesus doesn't want us to fight and argue. He doesn't want us to always want *our* way — to "be first."

If we share, everybody can have a good time. Everybody will be happy, just like my mobile.

Hebrews 13:16

And do not forget to do good and to share with others, for with such sacrifices God is pleased. *(NIV)*

#26

WHAT KIND OF AN ADVERTISEMENT ARE YOU?

Witnessing

(Hold up for the children a magazine showing a full page ad for an automobile.)

Who can tell me what this is? Yes, of course, it's a picture of an automobile. It's a *(Brand name)*. Isn't it beautiful? How would you like to ride home from church in this? But why is this picture of this car in this magazine? Why do they show pictures of beautiful cars on TV? It costs thousands of dollars to show them. They want you to see them and buy them. This is called advertising. If you have something good to sell, it's very important to advertise, and you have to make what you are selling look as good as you possibly can.

Suppose this were a picture of a kind of rusty car, with black smoke coming out of the exhaust pipe and a lot of oil dripping from the bottom — you would think, "Boy, I surely wouldn't buy *that* car." That would be bad advertising.

But why am I telling you this? You're not advertising, are you? *(Wait for answer.)* Oh, yes, you are. You advertise every day. All of us do. Did you know you advertise for your mom and dad? Sometimes by the way you act and the way you play, you tell people what your parents are like. They may say, "He's such a swell little boy — he must have wonderful parents." You see, *you* would be a *good* advertisement.

Do you know you even advertise for Jesus? You can be a good ad or you can be a poor one. If you love Jesus and try to please him, people will think nice things about Jesus, nice things about our church. People can't see Jesus. He doesn't advertise in magazines. People can only see us. So Jesus uses people like you and me. We advertise for him. Boy, we surely want to be good ads for Jesus, don't we?

Matthew 5:16

Let your light shine before men, that they may see your good deeds and praise your Father in heaven. *(NIV)*

#27

THE BEST BARGAIN — EVER

Giving

Did you ever hear your dad say that a dollar doesn't go as far as it used to? What do you suppose he meant by that? That he couldn't throw it as far as he did when he was a kid like you? George Washington, our first president, once threw a silver dollar across the Potomac River — that was pretty far.

What your dad meant was that a dollar won't buy as much as it did five or six or ten years ago. *(Relate and adjust the following statement to whatever parent, grandparent, or great-grandparent it applies to:)* When my (   ) was a little girl, you could buy twenty ice cream cones for a dollar — now you can't even buy a Big Mac for a dollar. *But* there is still a wonderful bargain *you can get* for a dollar. Your dollar can go all the way across the ocean and work for Jesus. *(If your church has a missionary it supports, you should mention that here.)* Every penny and every dollar you send to the missionaries goes on and on and on, working for Jesus. That's the best bargain you can ever get.

II Corinthians 9:7

Each man should give what he has decided in his heart to give, not reluctantly or under compulsion, for God loves a cheerful giver. *(NIV)*

#28

THAT'S NOT REALLY YOU!

Accepting Others

(Provide a mirror. It should be at least 12" x 12".)

I've got something here you look at every day. Or maybe I should say you look *into* every day. It tells you if you need a hair cut or if your face is dirty. It tells your mom if her make-up is on right or if she is getting any gray hair, and she's glad when she's not.

I'm going to hold this up in front of you, and I want you to tell me whom you see. *(Do this and ask each one whom he sees.)* You think you see yourself? Are you sure? Oh, no, you didn't! All you saw was some skin. That's not you. You think it is you? Well, suppose I took your face *(Joe)* and put it on *(Sammy)*. Then I took Sammy's face and put it on you. *(Show exchange with hand motions.)* Would Sammy be Joe, and would Joe be Sammy? Would you have to exchange names? Exchange moms and dads? *No!* Your face doesn't make you who you are. It's just like a mask you wear every day. What you *are* is what you are in your mind and heart. It's what you are inside, not outside.

Did you ever not like some people because you didn't like the way they looked? Maybe you didn't like their color. Maybe you even thought they were kind of ugly. Oh, we should never do that. Did you learn this song in Sunday School? "Jesus loves the little children, all the children of the world — red and yellow, black and white, they are precious in his sight. Jesus loves the little children of the world."

That's true. Jesus does love all the children of the world. And we surely do want to love everybody that Jesus does, don't we?

I Samuel 16:7

The Lord does not look at the things man looks at. Man looks at the outward appearance, but the Lord looks at the heart. *(NIV)*

#29
DON'T SLAM THAT DOOR!
Forgiving Others

Did you ever have a door slam in your face? You were just about to go through and somebody slammed the door shut. *(If there is a door close by, storyteller should act this out.)* That's no fun, is it? You were right there, and bang! It closed right in your face. Now do you think anybody would ever close the door in his own face? That would be like tearing down the bridge that you have to cross over. Do you think anybody would ever do that? Yes, people do, and I'm going to tell you a story that shows you just how this can happen.

Let's talk about a pretend person named Joe. Joe had a friend named Charlie. They were very good friends. But one day Charlie did something really mean to Joe, and Joe was very mad. But later Charlie said, "I'm sorry, Joe, I shouldn't have done that. Will you forgive me?" But Joe was *so* mad, he said, *"No,* I won't! You did a very bad thing to me. You're not my friend anymore!" Do you know what Joe did when he said, "No, I won't forgive you"? He slammed the door in his own face.

Well, I can see you don't understand. So let's look at God's answer book. *(Read Matthew 6:14, 15.)* You see, God's word says that if we don't forgive someone, God will not forgive us. And if God won't forgive us, it closes the door to heaven, the door we want to go through. You see, when Joe said "I won't forgive you," he slammed the door to heaven in his own face.

So if we want God to forgive us, we have to forgive others, even if they don't ask us to and even if they are not sorry. This is God's way. This is what Jesus did. He forgave those who drove those spikes in his hands. If he could forgive them, is there anyone we can't forgive?

Matthew 6:14, 15

For if you forgive men when they sin against you, your heavenly father will also forgive you. But if you do not forgive men their sins, your Father will not forgive your sins. *(NIV)*

LIFE AS A CHRISTIAN

#30
THEY BOTH GOT THE SAME FOOD — WHAT HAPPENED?

We Reap What We Sow

(For this story, bring two pieces of fruit. We used two bunches of grapes. One should be very appetizing looking, the other very unappealing; but both should be of the same variety and, if possible, from the same bush or tree. Put these in a bag.)

Well, if you kids guessed for a thousand years, you could never guess what is in this bag. I've got two things. One you would like, the other you wouldn't. One is beautiful, the other is kind of — well, you'll see. Take a look at this. *(Show bad fruit.)* You surely wouldn't want to eat this, would you? Now look at this. *(Show good fruit.)* Mmmm — I'd like to eat this *right now,* but I guess I'd better not. How could they be so different? Both had the same mama, both came off the same tree/vine, both got lots of water, both got the same care. What happened? The water and the sap both came from the roots and flowed right up to the branch. Why didn't this one *(Poor one)* grow like this one *(Good one)*? Wouldn't this one take the water and food? Is that why it's so shriveled? Say, I just thought of something. Are kids like this sometimes? Do you ever hear kids say, "I don't like that food. Do I have to eat *all* of this? I'm too full to drink my milk." Then a half hour later they want a cookie. Do you know any kids like that?

You know, God has a lot of kids in his people garden here on earth. He has lots of good Bible food for them. Food for your mind and your heart. But maybe when their family is having devotions, they don't want to pray, or they don't listen while the Bible is being read, or they don't pay attention to their Sunday school teacher. Now they won't look like this on the outside *(Show poor fruit)*, but that's how they will be on the inside *(Point to heart)*. Each of you can be the kind of kid you want to be. We surely don't want to look like this when we get big, do we?

John 15:5, 6

I am the vine; you are the branches. If a man remains in me and I in him, he will bear much fruit . . . If anyone does not remain in me, he is like a branch that is thrown away and withers . . . *(NIV)*

#31

LOOK! THEY'RE SIAMESE TWINS!

Spiritual Nourishment

(Select two children of the same age, size, and sex. Rehearse this story with them prior to storytelling time. Care should be taken to select children who can be depended on to follow instructions and not use the occasion to show off for the others.

(The two children can be loosely tied together, or if a large shirt is available, they can put opposite arms in sleeves. In either case they should appear to be attached at the hips and shoulders.)

I've got an interesting story for you this morning. It's about Siamese twins. Siamese twins are twin babies that are born stuck together. Sometimes doctors can cut them apart, but sometimes it would kill them to do this, so they have to live that way, together, all their life. They have to do everything together.

But do you know something? Each of you is a Siamese twin. *(Wait)* Yes, you are. I'm going to prove it.

Each of you is really like two people. You have a body, that's one; and your mind is your other part. You can't see this part, but it's very real, and it's the *most* real part of you. It makes you what you really are.

Let's see if we can show you what we mean.

(   ) and (   ), will you two come and help me? We're going to pretend that they are stuck together like Siamese twins, but instead of two people, they are really only one person with two parts. (   ), you be the body, and (   ), you be the spirit.

Now, what does a body need to be strong and healthy? Food, rest and exercise. *(At this point, body child should be smiling and standing straight with head erect.)* Now what will happen to this body if we don't feed it, or if we only give it a lot of junk food, and if it doesn't get exercise and sleep?

(At this point, body child's head slowly droops, his smile fades, and his body goes limp.)

We are sure *you* know this, and want to be big and strong. *(Child then straightens up and smile returns.)*

Now, how about your spirit? Did you know it also needs food and exercise? Many people take care of their bodies, but they forget all about their minds and hearts. They are just as important as your body — even more so.

God gave you your mind and heart to be the boss of your body. They tell your body what to do, and what's good for it. You feed your heart and mind when you listen to God's word in Sunday school, read your Bible, and pray. You're also feeding it when you study in school. All this is good food. It makes our minds and hearts strong. You also feed your mind and heart when you watch too much TV, and read nothing but comic books. *(Spirit child begins to droop, has a smirk on face.)*

When your mind and heart get weak and sick, they can't tell your body what to do, and your body can begin to do a lot of bad things and get you into a lot of trouble.

So if you want to be *(Spirit revives)* the kind of person God wants you to be, all you have to do is give your mind and heart and body lots of good food, and God will do the rest.

I Corinthians 6:19, 20

Do you not know that your body is a temple of the Holy Spirit, who is in you, whom you have received from God? You are not your own; you were bought at a price. Therefore honor God with your body. *(NIV)*

#32

YOU'RE USING THE WRONG KEY

Wisdom

Let's have a little quiz this morning. Who can tell me what this is? *(Hold up a lock. Get a large one if possible.)* It's a lock? Yes, that's right. Now what do locks do? They lock up things? But how do you unlock them? You use a key? Really? Well, maybe *you* can help me. This lock is closed, but I can't open it. I used a key; I'll show you. *(Take key from pocket or use one on your key ring; not, of course, the right one.)* You see, it won't open it. What did I do wrong? It's a good key, and keys are supposed to open locks, so why didn't it? *(The answer you want is, "That's the wrong key.")* Oh, did I use the wrong key? Well, I'll try another. *(Do so, and this is the right one.)*

Say, look — it opens it. *This* is the right key. Do you kids know you try to open locks every day? Oh, they are not like this one. But they are kind of like locks. Every day there are things you want to have that you can't get; things you want to do, but you can't. It's as if they were locked and you are not using the right key.

Let me show you what I mean. Suppose you're playing outside and your mom calls you and says, "Come in here right away!" *(Say these next lines in a whining, very disagreeable tone:)* "Ah, you're always spoiling my fun. You never let me play. It's not fair!"

That's the wrong key!

The wrong key to open your mom's heart. But suppose you said *(This very sweetly)*, "All right, Mom, I will, but could I just play for ten minutes more? Then I'll come *right* in." *That's the right key.* Sweetness always softens moms' hearts.

(For this next part we used the name of a man in the congregation who was a particularly good Bible student, or you might use the name of a well-known Bible teacher. Following is the format we used. You may adjust it to fit your situation.

We asked this man how he got so knowledgeable about the Bible, and what the key was to being a real Bible scholar. His answer: "You've got to study, study, study." Arrange this with him ahead of time.)

You children know Mr. (   ). He's sitting right back there. I wish I knew the Bible as well as he does. He knows it almost as well as he knows his own name, from cover to cover. Mr. (   ), will you tell the kids how you got to be a Bible scholar? What is the secret, the key? *(He answers:)* "You've got to study, study, study!" Now, suppose I think that's too hard, that it would take too long.

Suppose I decide I'll just pray. I'll ask Jesus to give me all the Bible knowledge Mr. (   ) has. That's *the wrong key.* And if I should pray and ask God about it, you know what I think he would say? I think he would say, "Mr. (   ) is right; study, study, study." *That's the right key.*

Do you know some people think that all you have to do to get to heaven is to do the best you can? Of course nobody ever does the best he can, but people think that if they try to be good, God will open the door and take them in. But being as good as you can is *the wrong key.* It won't open the doors to everlasting life with Jesus.

Jesus is the door and he gave us *the right key.*

If you tell Jesus that you love him, tell your friends that you love him, and if you believe that Jesus was raised from the dead and lives forever, heaven's door will open to you because *that's the right key!*

John 14:6

I am the way and the truth and the life. No one comes to the Father except through me. *(NIV)*

#33

DON'T THEY KNOW HOW DANGEROUS IT IS?

God's Protection

You know, kids, jails are terrible places. You're locked up with a lot of mean, cruel, and wicked people. It's bad enough if you have done something wrong and deserve to be there. But suppose you didn't do anything bad. Do you suppose there are any people like that in jail? Oh, yes, in many countries of the world people are in prison just because they told someone about Jesus. Many missionaries are in danger every day of being put in prison or thrown out of the country, just because they are missionaries. The jails in those countries are horrible. Why do missionaries go there? Don't they know how dangerous it is? Sure they do. Why do they take those chances?

Because God told them to go, and so they went, just like the disciples. You remember Paul and Silas, how they got beaten and thrown in prison? What do you suppose they said when that happened? Did they say, "Boy, if this is the thanks we get for following Jesus, we're surely not going to follow him *anymore*"?

No, they surely didn't. They were thankful that they were able to do this for Jesus, and they started to sing. And you can be sure they didn't sing any sad songs. I'll bet the whole prison heard them.

You see, kids, if you're doing what God wants you to do, you can *sing,* wherever you are.

Acts 16:25

About midnight Paul and Silas were praying and singing hymns to God, and the other prisoners were listening to them. *(NIV)*

#34

YOU GOTTA HAVE A RESERVATION

Heaven

Have you kids ever wished you lived in a different house? Maybe one bigger or better than the one you have, with a big swimming pool or a ball diamond next door? Maybe you girls would like a house with a big three-room doll house in the back yard, big enough for you to play in.

But, you know, houses always need repairing and painting. The roofs leak. The plumbing gets stopped up. But couldn't God give us a perfect house? No problems and no rent to pay? Sure he could, but he doesn't want to. Why doesn't he want to — doesn't he love us?

Well, do you remember Abraham in the Bible? He was God's special friend. Abraham was very rich — richer than any king. But do you know where Abraham lived? In a tent! Couldn't God give him a palace? Oh, yes, but God didn't want to. God wanted Abraham to know that this world was not his home. He was just camping down here on earth; heaven was his real home. He was in a tent now, but one day he would be home with Jesus.

And God wants us, too, to know that we're just camping here on earth; heaven is our real home. But you've got to have reservations. People used to say that Peter was going to be at the gate of heaven just to make sure no one came in who wasn't supposed to; but if that were true, do you know the only question he would ask? *(Wait)* Do you know and love Jesus? If you're not sure you've got reservations, ask your Sunday school teacher. Then you can really know.

II Corinthians 5:1

Now we know that if the earthly tent we live in is destroyed, we have a building from God, an eternal house in heaven, not built by human hands. *(NIV)*

#35

ARE YOU GUILTY OR NOT GUILTY?

A Christian On Trial

Have you kids ever been in a courtroom? When you are older, you may get a chance to be part of a jury and help the judge decide who is right and who is wrong in a court case. Whenever someone is arrested, it is a jury's job to decide whether the one who was arrested is guilty or not, and the judge's job to decide whether he deserved to go free or go to jail. The one who was arrested can say, "I don't want the judge to decide. I want some people to." Then the judge will ask twelve people to help him. The twelve people are called the jury. Also, two lawyers will be there. One will try to show the jury that the one who was arrested really is guilty and really *should* go to jail. He works for the government, and he's called the prosecutor. The other lawyer tries to get the jury to believe that the man is innocent and should not go to jail. He is called the defense attorney. This is called a court trial. The jury listens to the witnesses — the people who know something about the crime. Then the jury decides if the person is guilty or not guilty. If the jury says *guilty,* the judge will ask the man to stand, and the judge will hit his bench with a wooden hammer and say, "Guilty — I sentence you to one year in jail."

That's how a court trial works. We hope none of you is ever arrested and has to come before a judge. But now listen very carefully, because this part may be hard to understand, and you little ones may have to ask your daddy or your Sunday school teacher to explain it. Did you know each of you is on trial every day? That's right! There is a judge, our Heavenly Father, who watches what we do, what we say, and what we think. He knows the law, because he wrote it. He will say we are guilty or not guilty. Then there is the prosecutor, the devil. He watches what we do, and he is always telling God how bad we are and that we should be punished. He hates us. Of course, lots of what he says is true. Then there are lots of witnesses who see us. The Bible says we're surrounded by a big cloud of them. We can't see them because they are spirits. Then there is our defense attorney, our Lord Jesus. He knows we are guilty, but he loves us; and if we will go to him and tell him all the bad things we have done and tell him how sorry we are — if we really *are* sorry — and ask him to forgive us, he will stand before God our Heavenly Father and say, "Father, I want you to forgive them. Do it for me, because when I gave my life on the cross, I took their punishment, so let them go free."

And do you know what? I can just see God striking the bench and saying, *"Not guilty!"* Isn't it wonderful to be a Christian?

I John 1:9

If we confess our sins, he is faithful and just and will forgive us our sins and purify us from all unrighteousness. *(NIV)*

#36
LISTEN! THAT'S THE WARNING SIGNAL
Conscience

Do you kids know what a warning signal is? Now suppose you have been doing something that your mom says you shouldn't, and she says, "If you do it again, you'll get a spanking." That's a warning signal, isn't it? There are a lot of others. If you have a smoke alarm in your house, it will make a loud noise if you have a fire. Your dad may have an alarm on his car, and if anyone tries to open the door without the key, the alarm makes a loud noise, warning people that somebody is trying to steal it. Your dog may bark like crazy when a strange person comes to your door. He is warning you. He is being a good watchdog.

But did you know God put a warning signal in you? And just like all the others, it's to protect you. God's warning signal is called our conscience. God gave us this. It's in our heart. It's very quiet. It doesn't make a sound, but we can hear it if we want to. Suppose your mom said, "I don't want you to turn on the TV when I'm not at home. Some of those programs aren't good for you." But the next day you didn't have anything fun to do, and your mom wasn't home. So you said, "Well, she probably won't mind if I just watch a little while." But something inside you said, "You shouldn't do it." That was the voice of your conscience. That was God's warning signal. You did a good thing when you listened to it. But suppose you didn't; suppose you kept disobeying it. Do you know what would happen? Pretty soon you wouldn't hear God's signal at all. It would get softer and softer every time you didn't listen.

So every time you hear that warning signal, every time you know in here *(Point to heart)* that you shouldn't, DON'T!

I Corinthians 10:13

No temptation has seized you except what is common to man. And God is faithful; he will not let you be tempted beyond what you can bear. But when you are tempted, he will also provide a way out so that you can stand up under it. *(NIV)*

SIN, CONFESSION AND FORGIVENESS

#37

YOU CAN'T PUT MAKE-UP ON YOUR HEART

God's Cleansing

(You will need a burnt cork or charcoal, Bible, mirror, powder puff, washcloth. Have these in a large grocery bag. This story should be told by a woman, although with some modification, it could be told by a man. As you begin, place bag behind you. As you turn your back on the children, reach into the bag, and using burnt cork or charcoal, put a good-sized smudge on your face. Then turn back to children.)

I've got something very interesting in this bag to show you. Why are you laughing? What's so funny? My face is dirty? It couldn't be; I washed it this morning . . . Are you sure? Where? Well, I'll wipe it off. *(You wipe your face, but with the fingers that are dirty, and in such a way that the smudge is larger.)* Now what's so funny? *(Get answer.)* I don't believe it. Well, I'll look for myself; I have a mirror here. Oh, you're right; it is a little dirty. Now what shall I do? This is kind of embarrassing. Well, we could turn off the lights; then nobody could see the dirt. But you need the light? I know what I'll do; I'll just cover it with make-up. Then nobody will know. *(Pat face with powder puff; do not wipe. Smiling)* How's that? *(Distressed)* It's no better? It's still dirty? Well, I'll just have to cover my face. *(Put paper sack over head.)* I can't see where I'm going! *(Remove; pleading tone)* Now what shall I do? Wash it? Why didn't I think of that? *(Wash smudge off.)* How's that? Is it clean? Good! I feel better.

Now why do you think I did all that? It was to teach us a lesson — to teach us that dirt on my face is like sin in my heart. Sins are the bad things I do that need to be washed away. If I say I haven't done anything wrong, I'm just fooling myself, because God says I have. See, it's right here in the Bible. For all have sinned and come short of the glory of God. Everybody has sinned. You see, I couldn't believe my face was dirty because I didn't *want* to believe it. But when

I looked into the mirror, then I knew it. When I look into the Bible, it's sort of like God's mirror, showing me what I'm really like inside. I mustn't try to hide my sin. That's just like trying to put make-up on my heart. It doesn't help to turn off the lights — God always sees me, no matter how I try to hide. But do you know, God made a way for my heart to be really clean. I don't have to cover it or hide it. All I need to do is confess, tell God I'm sorry for the bad things I do, and ask him to forgive me. And he will, and my heart will be washed whiter than snow.

I John 1:9

If we confess our sins, he is faithful and just and will forgive us our sins and purify us from all unright-eousness. *(NIV)*

#38
THEY'RE BIG AS GIANTS!

Obedience

Do you children remember the story from the Old Testament about how the children of Israel finally escaped from the land of Egypt, and all the years they spent crossing the desert on their way to the promised land?

Finally they came to the edge of the desert, to the hill country where the Amorites lived. They were evil people who worshipped demons. God told the Children of Israel that he was giving them this land, but they were going to have to fight them and wipe them out. But the Children of Israel were scared. They said, "Their army is too big for us, and some of the people look like giants. First, let's send spies to see if we can win." Moses didn't like this, because God said they would be able to wipe them out; but he said, "Okay, we will send twelve spies." Well, the spies went to the hill country, and they looked over the whole land. When they came back, two of the spies said, "It's a wonderful land, lots of food everywhere; we can easily defeat them. Let's go!" The other ten said, "No, we would never do it. Their soldiers are fierce, and some look like giants. Let's go back to Egypt."

That was a terrible thing to say, because God had rescued them from Egypt. Moses was very angry, and God was angry, too. He said, "Because you would not obey me, none of you adults will go into the Promised Land. You will die in the desert."

Then those cowardly Israelites changed their minds and said, "We will go, we will go." Moses said, "Don't do it. God will not fight for you." They did go, and the Amorites swarmed down on them like a flock of bees, and many of the Israelites were injured or killed because they didn't obey God.

Why didn't God fight for them? They were brave, weren't they, to fight such a big army? Doesn't God like brave people? *(Wait)* Yes, but most of all he wants people to obey him.

Remember, kids, you can do anything God tells you to do. But if you disobey God, *you* will be fighting giants. But if you obey him, a giant will be fighting for you. And you know who that giant is, don't you? Our Lord Jesus.

Jeremiah 7:23

Obey me, and I will be your God and you will be my people. Walk in all the ways I command you, that it may go well with you. *(NIV)*

#39

THEY ALL DESERTED HIM

Denying Jesus

Did you kids ever promise to do something, and then you didn't? Or did you ever promise you wouldn't do something, and then you did? Then later you were sorry you broke your promise? That happened to Jesus' disciples. You remember, it was at Jesus' last supper with them — Jesus was very sad and he told them that one of them would betray him.

Oh, how could they betray Jesus? But one of them did. That was Judas. Then later Jesus said, "The rulers are going to strike me and kill me, and all of you will run away." "Oh, we would never do that," they said. Peter said, "Even if all these guys run away, I never will." Jesus looked at Peter with love in his eyes. "Peter," he said, "before the cock crows, you will deny me three times." Later, you remember, the soldiers came and arrested Jesus, and all the disciples did run away.

Later Peter did come back to the building where Jesus was, and stood outside, warming himself by the fire. Someone came up and said, "You were one of his followers." Peter said, "No, I wasn't." A rooster crowed, but Peter didn't hear it. Later another person said, "You're one of his disciples." Again Peter said, "I am not." And again a rooster crowed, but Peter paid no attention. Later, a little servant girl, who was one-half Peter's size, said, "You're one of his disciples, I know." Peter cursed and said he never knew Jesus. A rooster crowed again. This time it was like a dagger stabbing him in the heart. "Oh, I denied my Jesus, I denied my Jesus." But Peter couldn't get to Jesus to ask forgiveness.

Later when they took Jesus to the cross, you remember what he said? "Father, forgive them, they don't know what they are doing." And when, with a shout, Jesus died — Peter was forgiven, and we can be forgiven too, even if sometimes we have denied Jesus.

John 13:38

Then Jesus answered, "Will you really lay down your life for me? I tell you the truth, before the rooster crows, you will disown me three times!" *(NIV)*

#40
STOP, THIEF!

Honesty

Let's pretend again this morning. Pretend you rode your bike to the market, you parked it in front, and when you came out it was gone. Suppose somebody broke into your house while your family was away and stole your VCR and all your mom's jewelry. What would you call a person who would do a thing like that? A thief! That's right. That's stealing, isn't it? The Bible says it's wrong — it's a sin.

Now, does it have to be something you can hold in your hand, something that costs money? Oh, no! Let me show you.

Whoever stole your bike could bring it back, or the police could catch the one who stole your VCR and jewelry and return it. But do you know that there are some stolen things that can never be paid back? They are gone forever. You would steal something, and no matter how much you wanted to, you could never give it back.

Let's pretend some more. Your mom has invited some old friends over for dinner. She is trying to finish a dress she wants to wear tonight. She couldn't do it earlier because she had to get the family room cleaned up. She still has one hour she can work on her dress. She says, "Please, please, don't you or any of your friends play in the family room. I'm going upstairs to sew."

But in a little while some of your pals come over, and you forget. And when Mom comes down later she says, *"Oh, no!* Oh, I could just cry — how could you do this?" There was craft paint on the carpet, play dough on the furniture, and 3,000 Lego blocks everywhere. You know what she would have to do? She couldn't sew; she would have to spend that hour cleaning up. Was there a thief in that house? Did somebody steal something? Oh, yes. You stole one hour of your mother's time. It belonged to *her* and *you* used it.

Did you ever think that you could steal anyone's time? That it's really stealing? It is. We are taking something that belongs to somebody else. We can steal our teacher's time, and we can even steal God's time — the time he wants to spend with us in Sunday school and church.

So you see, a boy or girl could be a thief and not even know it. And I know none of us wants to be a thief, do we?

Exodus 20:15

You shall not steal. *(NIV)*

#41

WHO WOULD DO THAT TO ME?

Broken Promises

(Provide a beautifully wrapped gift box that is empty.)

Look what somebody gave me when I came into church this morning. I should wait until I get home from church, but I just can't wait to see what's inside. It doesn't rattle. *(Shake it.)* It's not very heavy. It surely must be something special, wrapped as pretty as it is. What do you think it could be? It just says *(Looking at card)*, "Because I love you." What do you think I ought to do with it? Open it? Okay, I will. Are you as excited as I am? You would be if it were for you. *(Take time opening.)* Now — wait — look, it's empty! Somebody gave me an empty box. What kind of a present is that? It's empty. Boy, that's a disappointment. Why would anybody do that to me? *(Take a few moments to fold paper and place it in the box. Shake your head in disbelief.)* You know, I think I know why this happened. I think it happened to teach us a good lesson.

Do you know what this empty box is like? It's like a broken promise. This box promised me a gift, but it broke that promise; it was empty. When we break a promise, we give someone an empty box.

Did you ever break a promise? Did you ever say you would do something, and then you didn't? Did you ever tell your mom you'd be right home from school? You said, "Really, Mom, I will, I promise." But you stopped to play. A broken promise is saying something that's not true, and we know what that is, don't we? Never make a promise if you can't keep it. Jesus never broke a promise, and he made a lot of them.

Ecclesiastes 5:5

It is better not to vow than to make a vow and not fulfill it. *(NIV)*

#42
BUT WE DON'T HAVE TO ACT LIKE DUMB SHEEP
Waywardness

Have you kids ever watched a sheepdog leading sheep? Perhaps you saw it on TV. It's wonderful to see how they do it.

There can be a flock of one hundred sheep and only one dog to guard them. They all want to go in different directions, but the sheepdog runs around them, keeping them in one pack. *(With hands, illustrate this.)*

I wonder why the shepherd can't just let the sheep go anywhere they want to. It's a big prairie — what could happen to them?

Did you know that of all the animals God made, sheep are the dumbest? They are the most helpless. Unless the sheepdog or the shepherd leads them, they will always get into trouble. They will get lost, they will get caught in a fence, or eat poison grass, or a wolf or coyote might kill and eat them.

But why did God make them that way? He could have made them the smartest of all the animals, but he didn't.

Why do you think God called *us* his sheep? Couldn't he call us his leopards or his eagles? Why didn't he call us one of the brave, smart, or beautiful animals? Do you suppose he made the sheep that way, always getting lost, always getting into trouble, because he wanted to show us how *we* are?

That means we always want to go and do what we want, not what God wants. And when we do what we want, it's just like what happens to the sheep if they run away from the shepherd — they always get into lots of trouble.

Jesus, our good shepherd, laid down his life for us. He calls us his sheep, and that's what we are. *But* we don't have to *act* like *dumb sheep,* do we? We won't, if we always stay close to our shepherd.

Isaiah 40:11

He tends his flock like a shepherd: He gathers the lambs in his arms and carries them close to his heart; he gently leads those that have young. *(NIV)*

#43

NEVER THINK SOMEONE IS TOO BAD

Forgiveness

You know, kids, there are many different kinds of people in this world, aren't there? Some are very good, kind, and loving. I guess most are just okay. But some are mean, nasty, and cruel. You just wonder how they could be so bad. It surely wouldn't do any good to tell them about Jesus, would it? I'm going to tell you a story about two of the worst people you've ever heard about.

The first one went around hunting for Christians to be put in jail and killed. Oh, he didn't touch them — he thought he was too good. He just stood there and told other evil people what to do.

It surely wouldn't do any good to tell him about Jesus. The second man was even worse. He was a slave trader. Slave traders took their ships to Africa, where they captured people and chained them up like animals. They threw them in the bottom of the ship and brought them to England and America to be sold as slaves. They were horribly cruel to them. They gave them almost no food. If they got sick, they would throw them overboard to the sharks. It wouldn't do any good to tell them about Jesus either, would it?

Do you know what one of these slave traders did? He wrote a song. That's right. And let's just listen to it. *(Teller sings "Amazing Grace." He/she does not change tone of voice to give any hint of what is to come.)* What happened? How could that slave trader write a song like that? *(Wait)* I'll tell you how — he met Jesus. And do you know who the other man was I told you about? The one who was so cruel to Christians? The *Apostle Paul!* What happened to him? He wanted to kill the Christians! *(Wait)* He, too, met Jesus.

So, kids, never think anybody is too bad, too wicked. All they need to do is to meet Jesus.

(The song "Amazing Grace," should be done a ca-pella. It should be sung simply, by one who can make every

word understood.)

Romans 8:1, 2

Therefore, there is now no condemnation for those who are in Christ Jesus, because through Christ Jesus the law of the Spirit of Life set me free from the law of sin and death. *(NIV)*

#44

IT LOOKS LIKE CHICKEN SCRATCHING

The Right Prescription

Do you kids know what doctors' prescriptions are? Suppose you woke up one morning and you could hardly breathe. It felt as if somebody filled your head with a hot balloon, ready to pop. You were in a cold room, but you were perspiring. You told your mother you were too sick to go to school, but she thought you were just making excuses. "I'll take your temperature and see." *(Action of shaking thermometer and putting in mouth.)* She did, and the mercury — that's the stuff in the thermometer that goes up and down — shot right to the top. "Wow! 103 degrees! We've got to get you to the doctor right away!"

Well, the doctor *(Go through motions)* felt your pulse, took your temperature, looked into your eyes, down your throat, listened to your chest, then reached into his desk and took out a pad of paper. "Take this to your local pharmacy," he said. He wrote something on the paper that looked like chicken scratching or a foreign language. You sure hoped the drugstore man could read it and not give you something that was bad for you. Anyway, you knew it would look like cherry pop, but would taste horrible. *(Shudder)*

That piece of paper is called a prescription. It told the drugstore man what medicine to put into the bottle for you. So you took the medicine, went to bed, and in a few days you felt great again — all because you followed the doctor's orders and took your medicine.

We have a lot of names for Jesus, don't we? Lord, Savior, Redeemer, our Helper. Can you think of one more — one you would call him when you are sick? The Great Physician, the Great Doctor. He can heal all our diseases, especially when we are sick in here. *(Point to heart.)* Did you know he wrote out a prescription just for us, in our language? We can read it, it's not like those big words in a doctor's prescription.

It tell us what's wrong with us, and it tells us what to do

about it. One of the things it tells us is that we have a sickness called sin. We were born with it. Jesus is the only one who can cure it, and when we are sin sick, Jesus has just the right medicine. But, of course, we've got to take it. It doesn't taste very good sometimes. It says we've got to confess — that means to tell God we are sorry we did a bad thing. But when we do, and ask Jesus to forgive us, oh boy! We feel great again — all because we followed God's prescription.

Hebrews 12:11

No discipline seems pleasant at the time, but painful. Later on, however, it produces a harvest of righteousness and peace for those who have been trained by it. *(NIV)*

THE BIBLE

#45
IT'S A TALKING BOOK, REALLY!
The Bible

(Obtain a music box and a hard-cover Bible, which by its appearance does not suggest that it is a Bible. The music box should be the type that plays when the lid is lifted.)

(If possible, use a mike. The person using it should be out of the children's sight, but able to view the actions of the storyteller. If this is not possible, have someone sitting behind the children speak the "music box" words.)

Good morning, kids! Let's have some music before we start. *(Take lid off music box and let it play for a few seconds, then close lid.)* That's kind of pretty, isn't it? All you have to do is lift the lid and it plays for you. Let's do it again. *(Repeat, calling attention to the fact that as soon as you close the lid, the music stops. Open it again very briefly and close. Put it to your ear as though to make sure music has stopped.)*

Let me tell you kids about something a lot better than a music box. Did you know God has a talking book? That's right, he does. Just like a music box, it talks to you when you open it, and it stops when you close it. You can open it anytime, day or night, and it will talk to you.

You never have to wind it — it doesn't need a motor. God has put his power in it. This is a very special kind of book. It shows you how to be good, it tells you when you are bad. It tells a lot of exciting true stories about some real heroes. It tells you which way to go, and it tells you which way you'd better not go. It really talks to you. Now let me show you how it works.

(Hold Bible in front of you and open it at random, but try to open at Old Testament portion when helper reads there, and New Testament when this is read. Coordinate this ahead. Helper should read a few verses, beginning the second Bible is opened, and stop immediately when it is closed. Bible should be closed with a snap, and always in the middle of a sentence.)

Did you kids notice something? The talking book stopped talking as soon as it was closed. Let's try it again. *(Again open and read a portion, but close before completion of verse.)*

You see, God's talking book, the Bible, will only talk to you when you open it. Now let's try it once more. *(Repeat)* See? You can put your Bible on a desk or table, and it can stay there for a week, or even a month. It won't talk to you until you open it. You can even put it away until it gets all covered with dust and cobwebs *(Brush off Bible and blow dust)*, and the same thing happens — it won't say a word.

Now what does this show us? If you want God to talk to you, you've got to open his book and read it every day.

Psalm 119:11

I have hidden your word in my heart that I might not sin against you. *(NIV)*

#46
HEY, WHAT'S THAT BAD SMELL?
God's Living Water

Have you kids ever driven across the desert? If you were driving from Los Angeles to the high country of Yosemite National Park, you would drive through the Mojave Desert. If you did this in the summer, it would be blazing hot and you surely would want a cold drink and to go where it was cooler — but just as you were coming out of the hot desert, you would see a beautiful blue lake. It looks so cool, so pretty, you just have to go see it. You think maybe you could even go swimming. So after you've asked many times, your dad finally says, "Okay, we will just go see." You point out the sign, your dad turns off the highway, and soon you are pretty close. Because it's been so hot, all the car windows are open, and pretty soon you begin to smell something kind of funny. Then when you get closer to that beautiful lake, you smell something really bad and you roll up the windows quickly.

This is Mono Lake. Mono Lake is a dead sea. Do you know why they call it a dead sea? Do you know why the water smells so bad? The water that runs into the lake is clear and fresh and sparkling. It comes from the snow-covered mountains just twenty miles away. It's snow water. It tastes wonderful — you can't find water that tastes any better anywhere. So what spoils that good water when it flows into the lake? It dies there because no water ever flows out. It gets water, but it never gives, and boy, it *really smells*.

Now this is why God wants us to tell other people about Jesus. He gives us his word, the Bible. It's called living water — the water of life — but God doesn't want it to stop in us. He wants it to go on and on. If we never tell anyone else, his word will die in us. We sure don't want to be like Mono Lake, do we? *(Teller should hold nose on last line.)*

John 4:14

Whoever drinks the water I give him will never thirst. Indeed, the water I give him will become in him a spring of water welling up to eternal life. *(NIV)*

#47

JUST LIKE HAVING JESUS IN YOUR MUD HUT

Bible Translators

This morning, kids, I want you to pretend you lived in a deep jungle far, far away. You had your own language, but nobody outside your tribe spoke it. Now there were some people living far across the world in America who knew about you and who wanted you to know about Jesus, just as they did. So they flew across the ocean, rode in a jeep for two days, took a riverboat, and finally got to your village. Of course they couldn't talk to you because they couldn't talk your language. So they built themselves a mud-brick house and began to know you and learn the language you speak.

As soon as they learned, they told you about Jesus and showed you the book that spoke Jesus' words. You couldn't read it because it was in the missionaries' language. But the missionaries said that if you would help them, they would write down the words in your very own language. So every day the missionary sat in your mud-brick house. He told you what the Bible said, and you told him how to say it in your language. This took a long, long time because the missionary had to be careful to say just what God said in his book. Maybe it took two years, maybe five, but finally it was done; you had your very own Bible — it talked to you. You were so happy, you wanted to take it everywhere. It was just like having Jesus in your mud-brick house. It was your treasure.

Now if those people way across the water, deep in that jungle, two weeks away from a road, a car, a TV, or a telephone were that happy about being able to read their Bible, wouldn't you think that all of us would want to read it every day? Because we want Jesus to be in our houses, just as he is in those mud huts in the jungle.

Proverbs 25:25

Like cold water to a weary soul is good news from a distant land. *(NIV)*

#48

WHAT DID YOU PUT
IN THE BANK TODAY?

Remembering Scripture

You know, kids, cars cost a lot of money, don't they? Let's pretend that your dad has been saving for a new car for a long time, and finally he has enough money. So he says, "Let's go down to the car dealer and pick one out." So you go. You like the blue one, your mom likes the beige one, but your dad says, "We'd better get the black one." So your dad signs all the papers, and makes out a check for the price, and your family has a spanking-new car.

But why did they give your daddy a car when all he gave them was a check, a piece of paper? Well, that check gave the car company the permission to go to your daddy's bank and take out enough money to pay for the car. That's how checks work. But of course they could only do that if your daddy first put the money in his bank account.

Did you kids know that each of you has a bank account, and you carry it with you every day? Every day you put things into that account. You look as though you don't believe me. Okay, I'll show you. *(Child)*, how much is 6 plus 15? That's right! What is the capital city of *(Your state)*? That's right, too. Now how did you know that? Why could you do that arithmetic problem? Because in school you put the answer in your mind-bank account when you studied, so you could draw it out when you needed it, just the way your daddy drew out the money for his car. Now, who can finish this: "For God so ——." Good. You could do *that* because in Sunday school you learned it, and then you put it in your mind bank. *(Point to head.)*

Thousands of years ago, King David said, "Your word have I hid in my heart, so I won't sin against you." David had God's word hidden in his mind and heart bank so he wouldn't sin against God. So you see, each of us has a bank account. One in our mind, and one in our heart, and we should put something good in our bank account every day.

II Timothy 3:15

From infancy you have known the holy Scriptures, which are able to make you wise for salvation through faith in Christ Jesus. *(NIV)*

#49

IT'S GOTTA GO THROUGH — NO MATTER WHAT

Sharing God's Letters

Let's pretend again this morning. Let's pretend you lived in St. Joseph, Missouri, over 100 years ago, and you had a very important letter you wanted to send to Sacramento, California. Well, you would go to your neighborhood letter-box and drop it in. Pretty soon a Dodge mail truck would come by and take it to the post office. It would go through their automatic canceling machine, and then another truck would take it to the airport where it would be loaded on a 747, and ZOOM! It would fly to California. Is that what would happen? Oh, no! Not 100 years ago. You would take it to the pony express station. It would be in a building that looked more like a small barn. You'd see some horses that looked like race horses and some riders that weren't much bigger than some of you are. A man would take your letter and put it in a leather pouch hanging on the horse's saddle. As soon as there were enough letters, the rider would jump onto the saddle, the gate would be opened, and he would ride like the wind — one mile, two, three, four five, six, seven, eight, nine, ten.

Coming to another pony express station, the rider would jump off that horse and jump on another, and again he'd go flying ten miles more. For 50 miles he would do this, before another rider would take his place. No matter what time of day, if it was hot or cold, if it was raining or snowing, on and on they raced to California, through Indian country, where the Indians hated the white man for stealing their land.

Why did they go so fast, work so hard, and take such chances? Because the mail had to go through, no matter what!

Suppose it were really hot one day in your neighborhood, and the air conditioner was broken in the post office near your house. Do you suppose the postmaster would say,

"Oh, it's too hot to work hard; let's take it easy. Maybe we should quit early. If the mail doesn't get out today, that's all right — one or two days won't matter." No, sir, no matter how hot it is, the mail has to go through, no matter what!

Do you kids have any mail to deliver? Oh, yes, you do. And so does everybody else in this church. It's the most important mail we will ever deliver.

Did you know that most of the books in the New Testament are letters from God? They are letters about his son Jesus — letters he wants us to read and then give to everybody we can, everywhere. The whole Bible is God's love letter to us and everybody on earth. God does not have any postmen but us, and we surely want his mail to go through, don't we? No matter what!

Matthew 28:19, 20

Therefore go and make disciples of all nations, baptizing them in the name of the Father and of the Son and of the Holy Spirit, and teaching them to obey everything I have commanded you. *(NIV)*

#50

HEY, WHO'S PULLING ME?

The Bible — Our Compass

(You will need a compass and a magnet.)

I have something in my hand that's very stubborn. It always wants to do something in just a certain way. Do you know anybody like that? No, this is not a person. He would have to be very little to fit in my hand, wouldn't he? *(Show the compass.)* Do you know what this is? Yes, it's a compass, and just as I said, it's stubborn. It won't point any way but north. See that needle? It's pointing north. Now I'll just turn this compass and see if we can fool it. *(Turn one-quarter.)* Look at that. The compass is turned, but that needle still points north. Let's try it again. *(Turn one-half.)* It's still pointing north.

Now what do we use compasses for? Well, anyone hiking in the jungle surely needs one. You would get lost and never find your way out without a compass. If you were fishing on the ocean and a heavy fog came up, so heavy you couldn't see the land, you could make a mistake when you were coming back and end up in the middle of the ocean if you didn't have a compass.

You know, the Bible is sort of like a compass. God gave it to us so we could always find our way to him. Do you know how it does this? It always points to Jesus. Thousands of years ago, before Jesus was born, God sent prophets to lead his people. And do you know what? They also pointed to Jesus. Now, is there anything that can fool this compass and make it point some other way except north? *(Wait)*

Oh, yes. Now watch. *(Demonstrate how a magnet works picking up a metal object, if you think the kids do not know.)* If I take this magnet and hold it here, the compass needle will be drawn to this magnet. It will point to this magnet and not north.

God's word says we can be drawn away from Jesus if we are not careful. Just as this magnet did, lots of things can pull us away — too much TV, or not coming to Sunday school. Anytime you realize that Jesus isn't as special to you as he once was, or you are doing or saying things you shouldn't, that's the time to *watch out*. There's a bad magnet somewhere.

James 4:8

Come near to God and he will come near to you. Wash your hands, you sinners, and purify your hearts, you double-minded. *(NIV)*

HOLIDAYS AND SPECIAL USE

#51

A BETTER TRADITION
THAN PUMPKIN PIE

Gratitude for God's Love (Thanksgiving)

Let's play a little game this morning. Let's close our eyes and imagine what we'll have for dinner on Thanksgiving day. Mmmm . . . What will you eat on Thanksgiving? *(Points to different children.)* Yummy turkey? Homemade dinner rolls? Pumpkin pie with whipped cream on top? What's your favorite Thanksgiving food? *(Get as many different answers as you can.)*

Do you kids know why we always have turkey and all the trimmings for Thanksgiving? What if we all ate pizza? Or peanut butter sandwiches? That would seem funny, wouldn't it? We always have turkey and stuffing and pumpkin pie because it's a tradition.That means it's been done over and over so much that turkey and pumpkin pie are what you look forward to every Thanksgiving. I'll bet your grandma, and her grandma, and even *her* grandma all had turkey on Thanksgiving Day.

I know an even better tradition than having turkey and pumpkin pie every Thanksgiving. Can you guess? It's having God love us, every day of the year. It's almost a tradition. He's loved your grandma, and her grandma, and even her grandma, and all the people in the world that ever lived. That's something to be thankful for on Thanksgiving and all year 'round, isn't it?

Psalm 107:1

Give thanks to the Lord, for he is good; his love endures forever. *(NIV)*

#52

WE WOULD HAVE TO BECOME ONE OF THEM

The Incarnation (Christmas)

Do you kids have any ants in your yard? Ants are very interesting insects. It would be fun if we could talk to them. There are a lot of questions I'd like to ask. I'd ask them: Why are you always so busy? Why do you walk so fast? Why do you touch your feelers to the other ants you pass? But you can't ask them because they couldn't answer back. And you know, there are some questions they might like to ask you, such as, "Why are you so big and why are we so small? Why do you step on me when I'm minding my own business? Why does your mom get so mad when we come in your house? We only want something to eat; we don't eat much." But we can't talk to them. Suppose I wanted to, wanted to real bad, wanted them to know me. What would I have to do? *(Wait)*

I'd have to become an ant, wouldn't I? Then I could talk to them and they could talk to me. They could tell me their troubles and ask me to help them. They could know me if I became an ant.

Did you know something like that happened 2,000 years ago? God came to earth. He came as a baby. We call it Christmas. He came so we could know he was real, so we could know we are talking to a real person when we pray, so we could know a real person is listening — someone who was just like us.

When we ask him to forgive us, we know he will because he promised. He came to earth to tell us that. You can't talk to an ant. They can't talk to you. But you can talk to Jesus *anytime.*

John 1:14

The Word became flesh and made his dwelling among us. We have seen his glory, the glory of the One and Only, who came from the Father, full of grace and truth. *(NIV)*

#53
NO ROOM — GO SOMEWHERE ELSE
Jesus in the Manger (Christmas)

I am going to tell you a story about something that happened a long, long time ago. When I am done I want you to tell me if the story is true. It's a story about a wonderful lady who was going to have a baby. But she and her husband were not worried that they had to travel to another town just when their baby was going to be born, because they knew there would be a doctor going along with them. They knew, too, that they would be riding on a donkey cart with soft rubber tires, and there would be lots of people along the way to help them because they knew how special she was. When they got to the town where they were going to stay, all the motel managers would rush out in the street shouting, "Stay in my motel!" — "Mine is best!" — "We've got nice soft beds!" — "Reduced winter rates!" They all wanted them in their motel, and all the important people in town came out to welcome them.

Now, is this a true story? Is this what really happened? Oh, no! We are talking, of course, about the Virgin Mary, the mother of Jesus. We don't know how she got to Bethlehem. Maybe she walked, and probably with nobody to help her but Joseph, her husband.

She had no doctor, and nobody thought she was special. When they finally got to Bethlehem, all the innkeepers said, "No room!" "Go somewhere else!" But finally, somebody let them sleep in their cow barn. That was their motel room — a dirty, smelly stable. Oh, you see lots of pictures of mangers on Christmas cards. They look pretty, but Jesus' crib didn't look like that, because cows, sheep and goats are dirty animals and they smell. There were rats and mice and flies where Jesus was born.

(An incredulous tone here) But he was God's Son! He was a prince! Why didn't God let Jesus be born in a palace? Why weren't there thousands of people there shouting, "A

King is born! A King is born!'"? Do you know who the only people who came to the manger were? Just some shepherds — the least important people in the whole country.

Do you know why God let Jesus be born this way? So that the poorest people in all the world, the people whom nobody loves or cares about, would know that Jesus came for them, too, and also for you and you *(Pointing to each child)* and you . . .

Luke 2:6, 7

The time came for the baby to be born, and she gave birth to her firstborn, a son. She wrapped him in cloths and placed him in a manger, because there was no room for them in the inn. *(NIV)*

#54
THE MOST BEAUTIFUL MOTEL EVER!
Jesus Makes Everything Beautiful (Christmas)

Do you kids like to travel? When you do, do you stay in motels? Did you ever stay in a very expensive one? Just for fun, I'd like to sometime, but I don't think I ever will. Do you know that some motels and hotels are so fancy, they cost more than $250.00 a night? They are beautiful — more like a room in a castle — with a king-size bed that's so pretty, you'd almost be afraid to sleep in it.

But do you know about the most beautiful motel room that ever was? I'll tell you.

One day, a long, long time ago, an angel came to a young girl named Mary. He told her she was going to have a baby, and that her baby would be the Son of God, the Savior of the world.

Mary was frightened. But the angel said, "Don't be afraid, Mary." So Mary said, "Whatever the Lord wants is okay with me." That's a really good thing for all of us to say. Mary and her husband Joseph waited nine long months, but then the Roman government said she had to go to her home town, Bethlehem, to be taxed. Well, Mary and Joseph started out. Mary rode on a donkey, even though her baby was due to be born any minute. I'm sure lots of times Mary prayed, "Oh, Lord, don't let my baby be born until we get to the inn!" (That's what they called motels.) "Don't let my baby be born on the side of the trail!"

Finally they could see the inn, and Mary was so happy! When they got there, Joseph went up to the inn door. *(At this point I went to one of the doors up front and knocked. The door opened and the "innkeeper" stuck his head out and said, "No room! No room! and shut the door. I knocked again and he said, "I told you — we're full! Go away!")* Joseph said, "But my wife is pregnant and our baby is due any moment — can't you find us a space somewhere?" *(Innkeeper says: "Well, there's a stable in back — you can go there." Door slams.)*

(Storyteller continues.) So Mary and Joseph went into the stable and made a bed in the straw. That night, Jesus was born in the most beautiful motel room that ever was.

Why was that room beautiful? Because Jesus was there! Jesus makes everything beautiful. If Jesus is in your home, it's a beautiful home. If Jesus is in your heart, you are beautiful — even if you look like me!

I Peter 2:9

But you are a chosen people, a royal priesthood, a holy nation, a people belonging to God, that you may declare the praises of him who called you out of darkness into his wonderful light. *(NIV)*

#55
LOOK WHO CAME TO THE GAME!
The Unexpected Guest (New Year's Day)

Well, are you kids going to watch the Rose Bowl Parade on TV on New Year's Day? Or maybe one of the bowl games? If Jesus came back to earth on that day, where would he go? To see the parade? Or to watch a football game? Would anybody pay any attention to him? Would they cheer for him? Think he was a star? Would any of the football teams want him to be the coach? Do you think the people at the Rose Bowl Parade would realize that he made every one of those million flowers? Do you know that people stay up all night long just to have a place to stand on the curb to watch the parade? Do you think they would do that just to see Jesus?

Do you realize that something very special is going to happen at 12 midnight? As soon as that clock strikes 12, God is going to give you a wonderful present. At the stroke of 12, God is going to give us a *brand new year!* If we ask him to, he will forgive every sin of last year — and *forget them.*

If we follow Jesus, our lives can be more beautiful than anything you'll see at a Rose Bowl Parade. And if we ask Jesus to be our coach, we'll make a lot of spiritual touchdowns — and he will help us to not commit so many fouls. At midnight, God is going to blow the whistle to start the game 19 - -. Let's all play on Jesus' team!

II Corinthians 5:17

Therefore, if anyone is in Christ, he is a new creation; the old has gone, the new has come! *(NIV)*

#56

I PROMISE NOT TO HIT MY LITTLE SISTER

New Year's Resolutions

(You will need a chalkboard and chalk for this story.)

(Date) was New Year's Day.

Do you kids feel any older? You don't? You look older. Did you make any New Year's resolutions? Do you know what they are? Well, let me tell you. A New Year's resolution is a promise you make to yourself. You promise yourself that for the whole year to come you will do something you should, you won't do something you should not. That's a resolution.

Your mom may promise herself that she is going on a diet to lose ten pounds, or your dad might promise he is going to play with his kids for a half hour every day. That would be a good New Year's resolution. But what New Year's resolution could you make? What could you promise yourself? You could promise that you won't hit your sister, no matter how much she bugs you. Or that whenever your mom asks you to do something, you'll say, "Okay, Mom, I'll do it," and won't say, "Ah, do I have to do it *now?*" *(Sour look.)* Or you won't say, "It wasn't my fault." Or, "He hit me first." *(Use facial expression and tone of voice that expresses these.)*

These things we do that we know Jesus doesn't like, do you suppose he writes them down on a chalkboard? *(Hold up chalkboard. Draw line down center.)* Maybe the good things on one side and the naughty things on the other? *(Put a few wavy lines on each side to represent entries.)* Do you suppose he erases the board every night, or just when the board gets full? How could we get the naughty side of that board wiped clean? We surely don't want it to be full of things that Jesus doesn't like.

Well, when you are saying your prayers at night before you go to sleep, and you remember something you did that you know you shouldn't have, right then say, "Jesus, I'm sorry I did that bad thing; will you forgive me?" Do you know what he will do? He will wipe the chalkboard of our hearts spanking clean. *(Erase "bad" side.)* The Bible says, "If we confess our sins, Jesus will forgive our sins." He won't remember them *anymore.* Isn't that wonderful!

Now let's all make some good New Year's resolutions, shall we? And tonight, remember this chalkboard.

Psalm 103:12

As far as the east is from the west, so far has he removed our transgressions from us. *(NIV)*

#57

DO YOU WANT TO BE GREAT?

Humility (Palm Sunday)

I'm going to tell you a story about two animals this morning. These two animals were just like some people we know. One was a donkey and the other was a stallion, and they lived in the same stable. The stallion was very proud that he was so big and strong. When people came by, they would say, "What a beautiful horse that is." Oh, this made him even more proud, and he walked around with his nose up in the air. *(Do so.)* He always made fun of the donkey because nobody thought he was beautiful — except maybe his mama. The stallion was hard to ride, because he always wanted to go his way instead of the way the rider wanted him to go. The donkey was not like that. He'd go wherever you wanted him to. He'd pull a plow, a wagon, or whatever you wanted. He figured that's what donkeys were for. He kind of wished he could do something great sometime, but he really didn't think he ever would.

Now the stallion and the donkey heard a very special person needed an animal to ride to Jerusalem. The stallion knew they would choose him. He said, "Oh, they'd never choose you, you're just a donkey." The donkey knew that, too. So the next day some people came into the stable and they looked at both of them. Then they said, "We want that one." *(Wait)* Now who do you think they chose? *(Wait)* Right, the donkey. And who do you think was going to ride on him? *(Wait)* Right again; it was Jesus! The donkey was going to carry Jesus on that very first Palm Sunday morning.

As they rode through the streets, people scattered palm branches in the way. They shouted, "Hosanna! Blessed is he who comes in the name of the Lord!" And that little donkey, who thought that he would never be anybody, and would never do anything important — here he was, carrying the King of Kings, our Lord Jesus.

Why do you suppose they chose him instead of that

beautiful stallion? Well, they could depend on the donkey to do what he should.

Did you know that's the way to be great? God doesn't need beautiful people — big people — and he can't use proud people at all. But if you do what God wants you to, go where he wants you to, and say what he wants you to — God can do great things with you.

Luke 1:52

He has brought down rulers from their thrones but has lifted up the humble. *(NIV)*

#58

HE'S ALIVE! HE'S ALIVE!

The Resurrection (Easter)

Today is Easter, and yet I'm going to tell you a story about a great enemy. It's an enemy everyone is afraid of, and everyone tries to hide from. If somebody told you that this enemy was at your front door, you would say, "Oh, no! Go away! I don't want to see you!"

But we should always start a story at the beginning. So we will go way back to the Garden of Eden. You remember how God told Adam and Eve that they could eat any fruit from any tree in the garden except the Tree of the Knowledge of Good and Evil? If they ate that fruit, they would have to die. But they didn't pay any attention to what God said. They listened to the devil instead. And when they ate that fruit, the great enemy came into the world. That enemy is death.

No one can defeat death, no matter how hard he tries. Everybody has to die — good people, bad people, kings, beggars, King David, Moses — everybody has to die. Back then, death was like a door that everybody was afraid to go through because they didn't know what was on the other side. They knew that once they died, they could never come back.

Then Jesus was born on that very first Christmas day. He was God's only son, the only person who never sinned. Could Jesus escape the great enemy, death? No, we know he couldn't. He died on that terrible cross so that we could be forgiven. And just like everyone else, he was buried. His disciples were so sad. Their leader and their teacher was dead.

But do you know what happened? *(Lots of spirit here.)* Three days later Jesus burst forth from his grave and *he was alive! Alive!* He rose from the dead! And we will, too, if we love Jesus. Do you know what death's door is like for everyone who loves Jesus? It's a door — that leads to heaven.

(For a more dramatic ending, if there is a door close by,

especially an outside door, when you say "that leads to heaven," swing this door wide and go through.)

Romans 6:8, 9

Now if we died with Christ, we believe that we will also live with him. For we know that since Christ was raised from the dead, he cannot die again; death no longer has mastery over him. *(NIV)*

ABOUT THE AUTHOR

Ted Lazicki has had a ministry of writing children's stories and plays over a 30-year time span — this while serving as Sunday school teacher, superintendent and church elder. This book is a sequel to his first book of children's sermons, *Something for the Kids.*

Several of his plays have been published, and many of his stories and articles have appeared in his denomination's (Church of the Lutheran Brethren) periodicals. Retired now from his secular position, he lives with his wife Fern in Arcadia, California, on his Lazy Z Ranch (a huge half-acre spread which mysteriously swells to five acres every time the grass needs mowing).

Of his six children, one son is a missionary in Chad, Africa, another son, a pastor in Eugene, Oregon. One daughter works with Frontiers Mission to Muslims in Pasadena, California. Two others are pastors' wives in Minnesota. The youngest daughter is a teaching assistant at Azusa Pacific University.

Ted is a volunteer for the building maintenance department at the U.S. Center for World Mission, where he is also the assistant editor of the *Global Prayer Digest.* At home, he reads, writes, and repairs. "We hike in California's High Sierra," Ted says, "and visit our far-flung children as often as funds and our consciences permit us."

If your church's children liked WHERE
DOES GOD LIVE? and would like another
year's worth of warm, funny "sermons",
you'll want to check out these additional 52
messages in the author's first book:

SOMETHING FOR THE KIDS

by
Ted Lazicki

Once kids have gotten used to a time in the worship service
reserved exclusively for them, they won't let it stop! Continue
the entertaining story-sermons they've grown to love at the
level they understand. You won't see any yawns as you relate
stories about the Route to Heaven, the Olympics and Being
a Christian, and Sand Castles and Eternal Life. They aren't
"preachy" — kids learn best by having fun. Even adults enjoy
eavesdropping on these humorous, simple, but meaningful
vignettes.

Sample titles include:

"Wow, What a Bargain!" (Everlasting Life)

"Did Adam Plant That Tree?" (God's Work)

"God's Phone Number" (Prayer)

*Full of fresh ideas for pastors, youth workers, or
anyone who loves children and wants to provide
something for the kids!*

ORDER FORM

MERIWETHER PUBLISHING LTD.
P.O. BOX 7710
COLORADO SPRINGS, CO 80933
TELEPHONE: (719) 594-4422

Please send me the following books:

_____ **Where Does God Live? #CC-B189**　　　　**$9.95**
by Ted Lazicki
Fifty-eight children's sermons for worship

_____ **Something for the Kids #CC-B192**　　　　**$9.95**
by Ted Lazicki
Fifty-two "front-row" sermons for children

_____ **No Experience Necessary! #CC-B107**　　　　**$12.95**
by Elaine Clanton Harpine
A "learn by doing" guide for creating children's worship

_____ **Storytelling From the Bible #CC-B145**　　　　**$10.95**
by Janet Litherland
The art of biblical storytelling

_____ **The Official Sunday School Teachers**　　　　**$9.95**
Handbook #CC-B152
by Joanne Owens
An indispensable aid for anyone involved in Sunday school activities

_____ **Teaching With Bible Games #CC-B108**　　　　**$10.95**
by Ed Dunlop
20 "kid-tested" contests for Christian education

_____ **You Can Do Christian Puppets #CC-B196**　　**$10.95**
by Bea Carlton
A basic guide to Christian puppetry

These and other fine Meriwether Publishing books are available
at your local Christian bookstore or direct from the publisher. Use
the handy order form on this page.

NAME: _____

ORGANIZATION NAME: _____

ADDRESS: _____

CITY:_____ STATE: _____ ZIP: _____

PHONE: _____
　❑　**Check Enclosed**
　❑　**Visa or MasterCard #** _____
　　　　　　　　　　　　　　　　　　　　Expiration
Signature: _____ *Date:* _____
　　　　　(required for Visa/MasterCard orders)

COLORADO RESIDENTS: Please add 3% sales tax.
SHIPPING: Include $2.75 for the first book and 50¢ for each additional book ordered.

　❑　*Please send me a copy of your complete catalog of books and plays.*

ORDER FORM

MERIWETHER PUBLISHING LTD.
P.O. BOX 7710
COLORADO SPRINGS, CO 80933
TELEPHONE: (719) 594-4422

Please send me the following books:

_____ **Where Does God Live? #CC-B189**   **$9.95**
by Ted Lazicki
Fifty-eight children's sermons for worship

_____ **Something for the Kids #CC-B192**   **$9.95**
by Ted Lazicki
Fifty-two "front-row" sermons for children

_____ **No Experience Necessary! #CC-B107**   **$12.95**
by Elaine Clanton Harpine
A "learn by doing" guide for creating children's worship

_____ **Storytelling From the Bible #CC-B145**   **$10.95**
by Janet Litherland
The art of biblical storytelling

_____ **The Official Sunday School Teachers**   **$9.95**
Handbook #CC-B152
by Joanne Owens
An indispensable aid for anyone involved in Sunday school activities

_____ **Teaching With Bible Games #CC-B108**   **$10.95**
by Ed Dunlop
20 "kid-tested" contests for Christian education

_____ **You Can Do Christian Puppets #CC-B196**   **$10.95**
by Bea Carlton
A basic guide to Christian puppetry

These and other fine Meriwether Publishing books are available at your local Christian bookstore or direct from the publisher. Use the handy order form on this page.

NAME: _____

ORGANIZATION NAME: _____

ADDRESS: _____

CITY:_____ STATE: _____ ZIP: _____

PHONE: _____
  ❑ **Check Enclosed**
  ❑ **Visa or MasterCard #** _____

Signature: _____ Expiration Date: _____
    (required for Visa/MasterCard orders)

COLORADO RESIDENTS: Please add 3% sales tax.
SHIPPING: Include $2.75 for the first book and 50¢ for each additional book ordered.

  ❑ *Please send me a copy of your complete catalog of books and plays.*